Home Plans for Solar Living

 **HOME PLANNERS, INC.**

23761 Research Drive
Farmington Hills, Michigan 48024

PRODUCED AND DESIGNED BY
THE COMPAGE COMPANY

San Francisco, California

Editorial Director: *Philip Alan Cecchettini*
Managing Editor: *Jessie Wood*

Writer: *Bob Beckstrom*
Illustrator: *Rik Olson*
Project Manager: *Alice Klein*
Designer and Art Director: *Joy Dickinson/Editorial Design*
Production Coordinator: *Samuel Jennings*
Consultant: *Southface Energy Institute, Atlanta, Georgia*
Typesetter: *Dharma Enterprises, Oakland, California*
Color Separator: *Southeastern Color Graphics, Inc.,*
Johnson City, Tennessee

HOME PLANNERS, INC.

Charles W. Talcott, Chairman
Rickard Bailey, President and Publisher
Karin Lotarski, Production Editor

PHOTO CREDITS

Front Cover	*Karen Bussolini, Greenwich, CT*
Back Cover	*Jack Parsons, Santa Fe, NM*
Title Page	*Robert Perron, Branford, CT*
Page 5	*Karen Bussolini, Greenwich, CT*
Page 6	*Top Robert Perron, Branford, CT*
	Bottom Michael Landis, St. Helena, CA
Page 7	*Top left, bottom left, Jack Parsons, Santa Fe, NM*
	Top right Derek Fell, Gardenvillle, PA
Page 8	*Top Jack Parsons, Santa Fe, NM*
	Bottom Paul Cleveland, Mill Valley, CA
Page 9	*Top Jack Parsons, Santa Fe, NM*
	Bottom left Michael Landis, St. Helena, CA
	Bottom right Karen Bussolini, Greenwich, CT
Page 10	*Top Robert Perron*
	Bottom Centerbrook Architects and Planners, Essex, CT
Page 11	*Derek Fell, Gardenville, PA*
Page 12	*Top Robert Perron, Branford, CT*
	Bottom Michael Landis, St. Helena, CA
Page 13	*Left and right Robert Perron, Branford, CT*
Page 14	*Top Jack Parsons, Santa Fe, NM*
	Bottom Michael Landis, St. Helena, CA
Page 15	*Top Paul Cleveland, Mill Valley, CA*
	Bottom Robert Perron, Branford, CT
Page 16	*Karen Bussolini, Greenwich, CT*

First printing February 1989

Contents

Homes in the Sun

WE ASK A LOT OF A NEW HOME. IT MUST SATISFY OUR BASIC NEED FOR SHELTER, of course, but we also look to it for comfort and beauty, to support our sense of personal identity, and to buffer the world around us. When we consider how a home meets these requirements, we look at many factors, such as the room arrangement, the overall size, the architectural style, and special amenities.

One important factor that is often overlooked, though, is whether the home is designed for living with the sun. Such a design includes attention to many details:

- It lets the sun shine directly into living spaces when it is wanted.
- It keeps sunshine out of living spaces when it is not wanted.
- It makes it possible to enjoy the sun at different times of the day in appropriate areas of the home.
- It takes advantage of the sun during different seasons.
- It uses the sun for energy to provide light and heat.
- It employs cooling techniques that do not rely heavily on expensive air conditioning.
- It provides convenient and attractive spaces for outdoor living.

A home designed with the sun in mind is energy efficient, but that is not its only benefit. The sun is not merely an alternative energy source. It can be a friend and companion, a source of joy and beauty. Consider these vignettes:

- Sitting in a rocking chair on a winter day in front of a bedroom window, basking in sunlight.
- Sitting in the shade of a cool porch on a hot summer day.
- Eating breakfast in a corner nook while watching the morning sun.
- Children playing games in a warm room flooded with sunlight streaming through large windows.

This formal dining room boasts a pleasant sitting area for daytime use thanks to a dramatic array of windows and skylights along the south wall. A sunspace, added to a larger room in this manner, brings the outdoors inside and enlarges the space at the same time.

- Eating a meal on a sunny terrace or deck in balmy weather.
- Eating a meal on a shaded terrace or deck in hot weather.
- Passing the open door to a sunroom on a chilly winter day and feeling the warmth pour into the rest of the house.
- From an upstairs balcony, enjoying the sight of sunshine pouring into the living room below through windows two stories tall.

This book shows how you can build a home that harmonizes with the sun. It gives you background information on solar architecture, shows examples of homes that use the sun, and presents a portfolio of home plans that take full advantage of the sun's benefits. The following gallery of photographs will give you a few examples before you delve into the details of solar architecture. These photographs present nothing new and exotic, but rather the classic and timeless style of homes in harmony with the sun. Relax and enjoy these photographs as you dream about how living with the sun can enrich your life.

1 *This home reaches for the sun in many different ways. From the rooftop collectors for active solar heating to the hilltop location, no possibility is overlooked for living with the sun. The longest side is oriented perfectly to the south, the large array of south-facing windows is protected by a roof overhang, no trees interfere with solar exposure, and the east wall has few windows.*

2 *Nothing compares with a deck for a versatile outdoor living space. This deck fronts the sunny south side of the house, inviting the outdoors in through large windows and glass doors. Spacious enough to offer both sunshine and shade, the deck also ties together and visually enlarges all the rooms on that side of the house.*

3 *Take a stroll in the sunlight, in the moonlight, in a snowstorm — this inviting corridor makes it all possible. Windows on both sides open this unusual indoor space to the outdoors as well as to the interior. Doors can be opened to warm the rooms when the corridor basks in the sun, or closed so the corridor can act as a buffer to the cold night air.*

1

2

3

5

4

4 Sunlight turns a simple bedroom into an inviting sitting room as well. With a south-facing window to let in light and warmth on sunny winter days, this is a perfect place to sit and read or carry on other daytime activities. The smaller window looks west to the sunset, filtered by the large tree outside, which also provides shade from the intense sun of summer afternoons.

5 This home fits so well into its parklike setting that it seems almost as natural as the surrounding greenery. But careful thought went into siting it just north of the tumbling waterfall, so large windows could be placed on the south side to capture sunshine as well as the serene view. The deciduous trees are just beginning to leaf and will provide shade in the summertime.

1 *Sunshine reaches deep into this living room through tall south windows, while the world outside is covered in snow. The dancing fire adds to the warmth and cheer, and with many comfortable places to curl up and relax, the room becomes a true winter haven.*

2 *Furnishings for a tropical lanai work in any climate when a large south window fills the room with sun. You can almost feel the gentle tradewinds and hear the lull of the surf in this warm and sunny sitting room.*

3 *The sun works its magic any time of day — whether warming a home with midday sunshine or casting a spell over it in the evening. Although window placement, site orientation, and energy conservation features are certainly the most critical considerations for a solar home, this Southwestern adobe, glowing in the sunset, demonstrates how shape, color, and texture can enhance the sun's effect in other important ways.*

1

2

3

5

4 Enclosed by a sunroom, this spa provides year-round outdoor living in an indoor space. Potted palms thrive in the spa's tropical atmosphere, bringing the outdoors inside. Plenty of winter sunshine, streaming through bay windows and skylights, helps to heat the space, and when temperatures fall at night or on cloudy days, the sunroom can be closed off from the rest of the house.

5 On a brisk winter day, the sun brings warmth and cheer to every surface it touches. This New England home is perfectly situated to take advantage of this free source of warmth. Most windows and a sunroom face south, and only a few bare tree branches obstruct the sun during the winter months. The same trees will provide shade from the afternoon summer sun.

4

1

1 *Living underground is sometimes the best way to live with the sun, as this bright and comfortable home shows. Earth berms shelter three sides, but the south-facing fourth side captures enough sunshine to make the interior feel anything but burrowlike. An overhead window scoops additional sunlight and warmth from the southern sky and directs it into rooms along the north wall.*

2 *A pool of sunlight makes a big splash in this luxury bathroom. Attached to the south wall of this home, it's the ideal place to enjoy a long soak on a chilly day. Large glass doors at the far end admit late afternoon sun and open onto a private deck with a shower and outdoor spa.*

2

3

3 *The outside of this Tucson home is planned as carefully as the inside for living with the sun. Bathed in winter sunlight, the entry courtyard greets visitors with a warm welcome, and when summer arrives, the deciduous tree's leafy canopy will provide a shady oasis from the hot sun. The wall to the left of the entry will also shade the doorway from late afternoon sun.*

1 *The primary source of heat in this room is not the blazing fire, but the surrounding beige wall. Called a Trombé wall after its French inventor, it uses the sun to heat the living space indirectly. With a bank of south-facing windows behind it, the concrete wall absorbs sunlight all day and slowly releases it into the room at night. It's a practical solution when the extensive window area necessary for direct solar gain would create problems, such as undesirable views, intense glare, or loss of privacy.*

2 *A dramatic architectural structure, this atrium brings daylight and garden views into unexpected places. Although not as effective for solar heating as a wall of south-facing windows, the atrium's window area can be sized to receive maximum direct sunlight at different times of the day.*

1

2

3

4

3 *This cheerful home in a woodsy Connecticut setting makes full use of the winter sun for helping to keep it warm. A wall of windows on the south side brings sunshine into a greenhouse on the ground floor, which can be closed off from the house at night. Higher windows admit sunlight into a tall open space flanked by bedrooms on the upper three floors. Windows between the bedrooms and sun-filled tower can be opened to let in warm air or closed at night so the space buffers the bedrooms from the cold outdoors.*

4 *In striking contrast to the south side, the north side of the home has only three small windows. The stepped dormers on the east side bring morning sunlight into each bedroom. Deciduous trees around the house will provide summer shade.*

1 *Throw open the doors and greet the sun! It's not just rustic charm that gives this classic Southwest home enough warmth to leave the doors open all day, even though there's snow on the ground. Tall windows take advantage of abundant winter sunshine, and thermal mass — in the form of tile floors, adobe walls, and masonry fireplace — helps to soak it up for later use.*

2 *Living with the sun sometimes means living without the sun — in the shade. And what better way to beat the heat than a graceful and roomy wraparound porch that allows you to find the perfect spot for staying cool, any time of day?*

3 *A remarkable setting and panoramic view are not all that make this home site overlooking San Francisco Bay extraordinary. Its solar exposure is ideal. The site slopes to the south, large trees protect the north and east sides, and there are no obstructions on the south side. The north side is primarily roof, with only a few small windows in the wall, while the major window areas face south and southwest to take advantage of vista and sun at the same time.*

1

2

3

4

4 *The brunch menu in this house includes a dash of bright sunshine, thanks to an eating nook in the southeast corner, generous windows, and skylights — all of which take advantage not only of solar opportunities but also of a green and expansive view. The tile floor in the kitchen provides thermal mass, helping to store some of the excess solar heat. In parts of the country where winters are severe or the summer sun intense, the skylight area could be reduced.*

Sunshine pouring in through two levels of windows helps to warm this bright, soaring space and complements the dramatic angles and planes of the vaulted ceiling. The light-colored floor, walls, and furniture all enhance the spacious, airy feeling of the room. This living room, oriented to the south, serves equally well as the hub of daytime activity and evening entertainment.

Living With the Sun

FROM ANCIENT CULTURES TO MODERN TIMES THE SUN HAS INSPIRED GREAT AND noble achievements. As an object of worship, mystery, and awe and as a source of art, investigation, and technology, it occupies a central place in human experience.

The sun also plays a major role in our everyday lives. Some ways are so obvious that we rarely think about them: the light we depend on each day, the warmth, the unfailing cycle of sunrise and sunset, the change of seasons, the daily weather report, our choice of vacation plans. Other ways are more subtle but perhaps more profound. When we are enjoying breakfast we seldom think about the complex food chain that begins with energy from the sun — in a sense we are eating sunshine! Our cars run on fossil fuels that originated with the sun. Much of our electricity is derived from energy sources that at some time were directly or indirectly connected with the sun. Even common expressions such as "sunny disposition" or "keep the sunny side up" suggest the sun's positive and pervasive influence.

As important as the sun is and always has been, it's surprising how many homes are built without taking it into account. Other factors, such as room arrangement, views, overall size, exterior style, and choice of materials and amenities, seem to play a greater role. These are important elements, but they should not overshadow the need to plan with the sun in mind. Overlooking the sun's potential benefits and drawbacks can lead to problems or inconveniences. For instance, a frequently used room such as the kitchen or family room may feel like a dark cave if it has only small, north-facing windows, while a seldom-used bathroom with a south-facing window basks in sunlight all day. Or a west-facing dining room may be too hot for comfortable dinners in the summer because it is overheated by late afternoon sunlight. Or a bedroom with large windows may feel chilly and uncomfortable at night. A home designed in harmony with the sun will minimize such problems and still be responsive to other important design concerns.

THE SUN'S INFLUENCE

In recent years, prompted by the need for more efficient energy use and the desire for bright, sunny indoor spaces, Americans have rediscovered the benefits of designing homes in harmony with the sun. Some of these designs, "solar homes" in the strictest sense, use the sun for as much as 75 to 95 percent of their energy needs by capturing, storing, and distributing its heat in various ways. Not all solar homes use the sun as their main energy source, but they do take advantage of many of its benefits.

There are two primary types of solar homes, active and passive. Active solar homes use mechanical devices to capture, store, and distribute heat. In passive solar homes, sunlight is admitted directly into the main living spaces during the winter and blocked by shading devices during the hot summer months; east- and west-facing windows are minimized and placed only where low, intense sunlight is desirable; the north side of the house is buffered from winter storms; and outdoor spaces are situated for the best solar exposure as well as for convenient outdoor living. This type is the more popular and is featured in this book.

Taking maximum advantage of the sun may seem to be the latest trend in home design, but it's an idea that has been with us for a long time. Ancient cultures all over the world knew how to manipulate the sun's energy for warmth, light, and cooling. They took into account the positions of the sun throughout the seasons in orienting the home, forming its shape, determining its size, and placing its openings. Many of these designs, when analyzed with modern calculations and precise measurements, follow with astonishing accuracy today's most sophisticated solar design precepts.

These ancient principles were used extensively until the early 1900s, when cheap energy and dazzling new ways to use it virtually eliminated the need to rely on the sun. Only in recent years, with volatile energy costs and an awareness of limited supplies forcing us to seek ways to conserve fossil fuels, have we again considered the sun in planning our homes. So in your own quest to live in tune with the sun you are following familiar, though faded, footsteps. Ironically, the more up-to-date your home is for today's trends and lifestyles, the more it is in harmony with ancient ideas and rhythms.

The sun is an abundant source of free energy that is amazingly simple to accommodate with sensitive design. But the most critical features of any home are not those that harness energy from the sun, but those that conserve energy, no matter what the source. The energy for heating, cooling, and electricity in any home must be used as efficiently as possible. Then, after energy-saving design and construction details are incorporated into the home plan, the potential for using the sun should be explored.

Passive solar homes offer many advantages. First, free energy from the sun helps you save on energy costs, which are a significant part of any household's monthly budget. Second, a passive solar home can be more pleasant to live in than an ordinary home. The spaces are bright and inviting. The rhythms of light and shadow set off architectural features, with sunlight itself becoming a friendly and playful guest. The heat produced by direct sunlight and by the surfaces it has heated can be more comfortable than ordinary forced air.

Third, the overall quality of design is likely to be high. Patterns of daily life through all the seasons have been carefully considered; energy requirements have been weighed; the effects of light and shadow have been evaluated. And an architect who is sensitive to solar potential is also likely to be aware of many other life-enhancing design factors.

Fourth, a home that is energy-efficient and enhanced by good solar design is more likely to sell in a sluggish real estate market. Buyers who are looking for long-term value recognize the savings in energy costs of a home that is partially heated by the sun and naturally cooled during the summer.

Finally, a home designed for living with the sun is likely to comply with building codes that prescribe energy-saving features in home construction. Many states and local areas have adopted energy codes in addition to their building codes. These codes specify requirements for insulation, type and size of windows,

Continued on page 22

A HOME IN TUNE WITH THE SUN

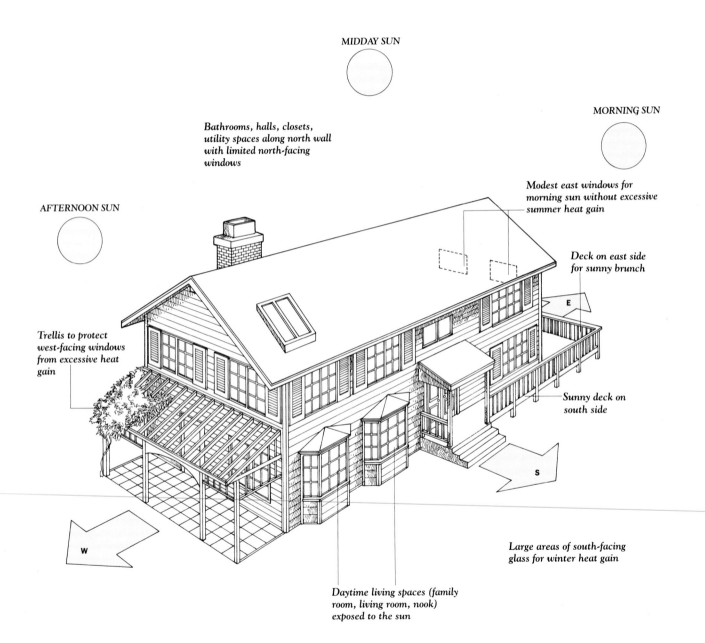

MIDDAY SUN

MORNING SUN

AFTERNOON SUN

Bathrooms, halls, closets, utility spaces along north wall with limited north-facing windows

Modest east windows for morning sun without excessive summer heat gain

Deck on east side for sunny brunch

E

Trellis to protect west-facing windows from excessive heat gain

Sunny deck on south side

S

W

Large areas of south-facing glass for winter heat gain

Daytime living spaces (family room, living room, nook) exposed to the sun

A HOME OUT OF TUNE WITH THE SUN

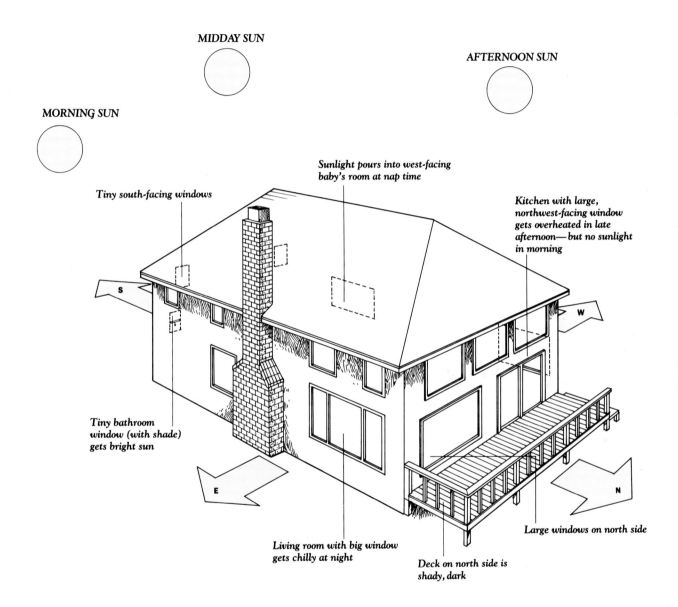

MIDDAY SUN

AFTERNOON SUN

MORNING SUN

Tiny south-facing windows

Sunlight pours into west-facing baby's room at nap time

Kitchen with large, northwest-facing window gets overheated in late afternoon— but no sunlight in morning

Tiny bathroom window (with shade) gets bright sun

Living room with big window gets chilly at night

Deck on north side is shady, dark

Large windows on north side

S

W

E

N

efficiency ratings for major appliances, and construction details for foundations, roofs, etc. When you build a home, you are responsible for making sure your plans meet these requirements. The home plans in this book will get you started in the right direction.

It may seem as though designing with the sun means a rigid plan with little design flexibility. Although this is somewhat true for site orientation and use of windows, you will see from the plans in this book that you have a great deal of choice in selecting a sun-oriented home. The plans present a wide variety of architectural styles. Not all of them make full use of the sun for heating and energy, but they all use the sun to make the interior spaces more livable, comfortable, and attractive.

To help you understand the plans presented in the "Portfolio of Plans," the first three chapters of this book are intended as a guide to the design principles and construction details of homes that live with the sun. If

you find a plan that is close to what you have in mind, you will be interested in the selection guidelines at the beginning of the portfolio. They include suggestions for adapting a plan.

The main thing to consider is exactly how you want to live with the sun. You may want a home where the bedrooms and kitchen capture early morning sunlight. Where spaces used during the day are warmed directly by the sun in the winter and shaded from it during the summer. Where the dining room is placed so that the hot sun of lingering summer afternoons does not overheat it, but views of sunset skies enhance dinners in wintertime. Where a terrace off the kitchen is bathed in warm sunshine on spring mornings but protected from burning afternoon sun during the summer. This book will give you fresh ideas for making such choices as you discover how solar living can enrich your life and add comfort, convenience, and appeal to your home.

Fundamentals of Solar Design

THE ENERGY CRISIS OF THE 1970S AND CONCERNS ABOUT THE GLOBAL CONSE-quences of air pollution have prompted countless experiments and design improvements to make homes more energy-efficient and less reliant on potentially limited fossil fuels. Designs range from futuristic fantasies and high-tech machines to a blending of classic home styles with modern energy-saving features. Many innovations focus on conserving heat, by adding more insulation to ceilings, walls, and floors, eliminating drafts and air leaks, installing high-performance windows that insulate three or four times as well as ordinary windows, designing open spaces for the free flow of heat, and burrowing homes into the earth. Other innovations focus on the more efficient use of existing energy equipment and devices: appliances and light fixtures that require less electricity, fireplaces that send heated air into the room instead of up the chimney, furnaces that burn fuel so efficiently that the flue pipe doesn't get hot, cooling systems that do not rely completely on air conditioning, and high-efficiency air conditioners and water heaters. A third group of innovations focuses on alternative energy sources, primarily wood for heating and the sun for heating, cooling, providing hot water, and generating electricity.

Many of these innovations are now widely used in homes. Others have proven less popular because of high costs, minimal benefits, or lack of design appeal. The widest-ranging experiments have involved techniques for tapping the sun's energy. Some of these techniques are unwieldy and impractical, but many can be adapted to a broad range of home designs.

Familiarity with these innovations and with the principles of passive solar homes will be helpful when you are choosing a home plan. The moment before you build is unique — you have options and opportunities you will never have again. It is not like buying a house that is already finished. Not all of this information will pertain to your particular situation, but the overall principles will apply.

Basic Solar Heating Methods

There are two basic ways to use the sun for heating your home. One is called active solar because it requires the action of fans, pumps, pipes, ducts, collectors, tanks, and other paraphernalia. Special collectors located outside the living space — often on the roof — absorb solar energy, which is then transferred, stored, and distributed as needed. Variations of this system are used to provide hot water.

The more common method is called passive solar. The term has been extended to include a number of elements in a well-designed home:

1. Proper location and size of windows, which are at least double-paned.
2. Thermal mass that absorbs sunlight and stores heat.
3. Shading measures to obstruct sunlight during the summer.
4. Ventilation measures to help provide comfort during warm or hot weather.
5. Ample energy-efficient features and equipment.

There are three basic styles of passive solar design for heating — direct gain, indirect gain, and the sunspace. *Direct gain* is the most common and most cost-effective style. Sunlight enters the living areas of a home directly through south-facing windows and is absorbed by features that provide thermal mass (a dense material that absorbs heat and gradually releases it) — for instance, a tile-covered concrete floor or a masonry wall. (See page 27 for a more detailed description of thermal mass.) The plans in this book are designed to feature many of the techniques of direct gain.

A variation of this method is called *indirect gain.* The sun shines in through the windows but does not reach directly into the living space. Instead, it is intercepted by a masonry wall or by water-filled containers placed on the interior side of the windows. The wall or water-filled containers provide the thermal mass.

Sunspaces, sometimes called solariums or attached greenhouses, are a third form of passive solar design. These rooms have large areas of south-facing glass and, to provide thermal mass, masonry floors or walls or water-filled containers. Sunspaces are maintained with minimal external heating and no air conditioning. Doors or operable windows provide for the flow of solar-heated air to other rooms in the house.

Sunspaces can be dramatic architectural elements and work well when designed properly. During the day, they are bright, sunlit areas that also collect solar heat to help warm adjacent rooms. At night they are shut off from the rest of the house so that heat loss is restricted only to the sunspace. When the sunspace is incorporated into a larger room and not isolated by separate doors, the extra heat loss may be accepted as

ACTIVE SOLAR HOME

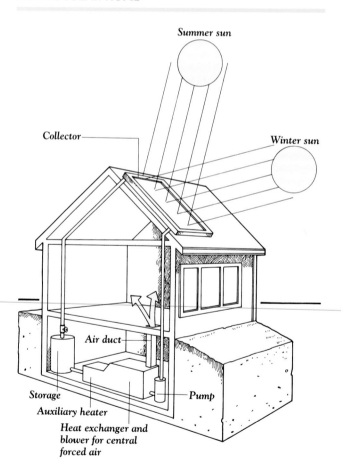

The sun heats fluid that is stored and then used to warm central forced air.

PASSIVE SOLAR HOMES: DIRECT GAIN, INDIRECT GAIN, AND SUNSPACE

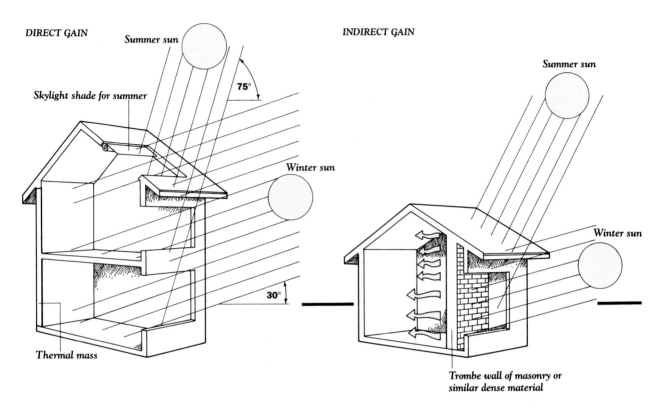

DIRECT GAIN

Summer sun

75°

Skylight shade for summer

Winter sun

30°

Thermal mass

INDIRECT GAIN

Summer sun

Winter sun

Trombe wall of masonry or similar dense material

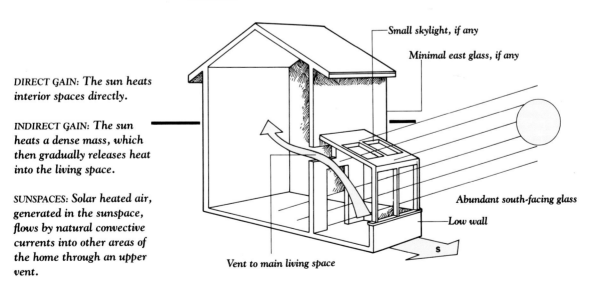

SUNSPACE

Small skylight, if any

Minimal east glass, if any

DIRECT GAIN: *The sun heats interior spaces directly.*

INDIRECT GAIN: *The sun heats a dense mass, which then gradually releases heat into the living space.*

SUNSPACES: *Solar heated air, generated in the sunspace, flows by natural convective currents into other areas of the home through an upper vent.*

Abundant south-facing glass

Low wall

S

Vent to main living space

HOW HEAT IS TRANSFERRED

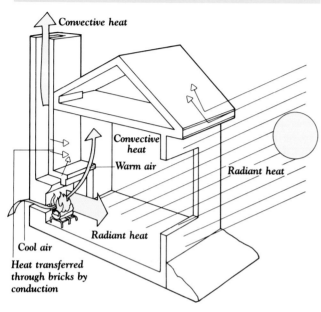

Radiant heat is direct; you don't feel its warmth if anything comes between source and receiver. Convection is heat transported by warmed air. Conduction is heat transferred through solid material, resulting in a surface that is warm to the touch.

PROBLEMS WITH TOO MUCH DIRECT GAIN

the price of the ambience. You need to be especially careful that the sunspace does not overheat the house during warm or hot weather. With proper venting, the sunspace can also contribute to summertime cooling by working as a solar chimney: hot air rises and escapes through the upper vents. (Sunspaces are described in greater detail in the section called "Special Features" on pages 72 – 74.)

A nice feature of passive solar homes is that they provide radiant heat, which occurs when an object receives warmth directly from a heat source without the air or surroundings needing to be warmed first. There are some limitations, however, to the ways in which you can use this free, abundant, and cheerful heat for your home.

Some Limitations

One limitation of passive solar heating is that heat enters the house only when the sun shines. If an obstruction (such as a wall, ceiling, cloud, or tree) comes between the sun and living space, the warmth is blocked. Of course, this principle can be put to good use in the summer by shading the sunshine from windows that would otherwise admit it directly into the house.

Another drawback is that solar heat is available for only a few hours each day and even fewer in cloudy weather. A third limitation is that the direct radiant heat only benefits people occupying the sunny rooms; it does not heat other rooms, at least not directly. It also requires that most of the windows be located on the south wall of the building to take full advantage of the sunny hours. However, other factors, such as views, privacy, or room arrangement, may make other window locations more desirable. Another problem with windows, compared with ceilings and walls, is that they are poor insulators and become heat losers when the sun is not shining through them. Therefore, passive solar homes must be designed carefully. Finally, if it is not managed properly with such devices as shades

(Left) Too much direct gain can cause glare, fading, and overheating. Too much glass can also cause excessive heat loss at night.

and overhangs, direct sunlight can create problems such as excessive glare, uncomfortable overheating, and fading of fabrics.

Some Solutions

Overcoming these limitations, or at least mitigating them, is the goal of passive solar design. Solutions include capturing and storing the sun's heat with the use of thermal mass, preventing overheating through the use of various shading techniques, and reducing the heat loss through large window areas.

THERMAL MASS.   If you've ever walked barefoot on hot pavement you know that certain dense materials absorb heat from the sun very effectively, especially if they are dark in color. Many of these materials are common in construction — brick, tile, concrete, and stone, for example — and can be used in the floors and walls of rooms where the sun will shine on them. This dense material, or *thermal mass,* is most effective when sunlight strikes it directly. A tile-covered slab floor directly inside a bank of south-facing windows is the essence of passive solar design. Other examples of thermal mass include a masonry wall on the north side of a room with south-facing glass, a masonry fireplace located in direct sunlight, or water-filled containers that support planting beds in a sunspace. These are all examples of direct gain designs. Indirect gain designs include a concrete wall or a row of water containers located directly inside south-facing glass. Some solar designers now believe that small amounts of extra mass, even in the form of extra plaster on the walls and ceilings, are sufficient for some heat storage.

SHADING.   Because sunlight streaming through a window is not always welcome, shading is an important consideration in passive solar design. South-facing windows are the simplest to shade because of seasonal changes in the angle of the sun. In the winter the sun

(Right) A roof overhang shades south-facing windows from the hot sun during early summer. Additional shading devices may also be necessary at other times.

TYPES OF THERMAL MASS

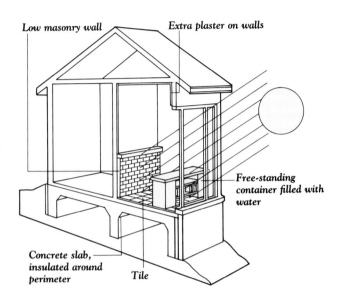

Low masonry wall   *Extra plaster on walls*

Free-standing container filled with water

Concrete slab, insulated around perimeter   *Tile*

SHADING SOUTH-FACING WINDOWS

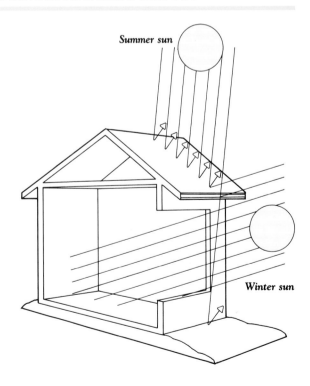

Summer sun

Winter sun

WINDOW INSULATION: MOVABLE INSULATION

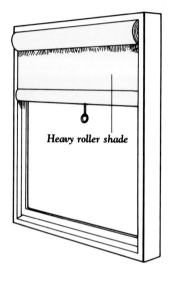

Heavy roller shade

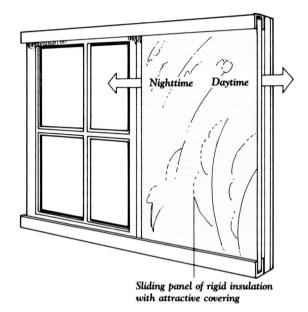

Nighttime   Daytime

*Sliding panel of rigid insulation
with attractive covering*

stays fairly low in the sky all day and penetrates easily into rooms with windows facing south. In the summer the sun swings high overhead during the middle of the day and is shaded from those same windows by roof overhangs or other devices. But windows facing east and west are difficult to shade with overhangs because the intense summer sun lingers close to the horizon in the early mornings and late afternoons. An overhang would have to reach out 6 to 10 feet to provide enough shade. Better shading is provided by screens, shades, porches, carports, trellises, or trees, but they have to be placed carefully so as not to block desirable views, breezes, and light.

REGULATING HEAT LOSS.   The problem of heat loss through windows is not as easy to overcome as the problem of excessive heat gain. Much of the valuable solar heat that pours in through south-facing windows can be lost at night and on cloudy days through those same windows. And windows on the north, east, and west sides of the house receive only a negligible amount of winter sunlight and lose much more heat than they gain. A balance must be achieved among many fac-

tors — the surface area of windows that admit solar heat and those that don't, heat storage capacity, insulation capabilities, comfort factors, and aesthetic considerations — in order to determine the right amount of window area for various exposures. Otherwise, benefits from solar heating are more than offset by heat lost through large glass areas.

The best solution to this problem is to have windows that insulate effectively. Double-paned windows, or storm windows used with single-paned windows, are a minimal starting point. Movable window insulation, such as thick shades or shutters, that closes over windows at night in winter and during the day in summer will increase insulation values. However, the inconvenience of having to operate the shades or shutters every day is a major drawback. High-performance windows appear to be a more promising option. Some use a type of glass called low-E, which has a microscopically thin heat-reflective coating to bounce heat back into the house in winter. Other window products, either on the market or currently undergoing research, use special gases between the panes or gel-like materials in place of glass.

WINDOW INSULATION: INSULATING GLASS

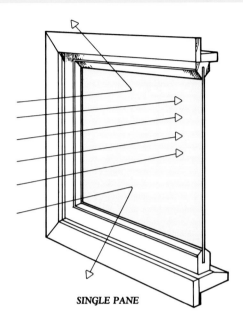

SINGLE PANE

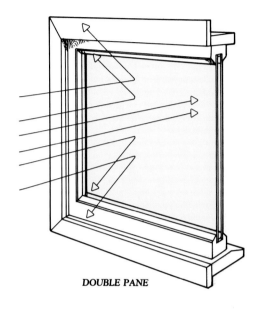

DOUBLE PANE

Overall Design

The overall design of the home plays an important role in maximizing the potential of solar energy. The best house shapes are those that have the longest wall on the south side. The rooms along this wall should be those used during the day, especially in the winter. Bathrooms, closets, and other auxiliary rooms can be placed on the north side where direct sunshine is not needed. Open plans, in which spaces flow together, help the heat to circulate more efficiently. And homes with compact shapes are more energy-efficient than those with sprawling, multiwinged floor plans.

Bringing all these factors into play and then balancing them with the aesthetic and functional needs of daily living is a complex task. Remarkably, the sun helps to solve some of the problems it creates. Seasonal changes in the sun's path (actually, changes in the earth's path) work to good advantage. When the sun is needed most for heating it traces a conveniently low arc through the winter sky, and in the summer it is easy to shade during most of the day. The sun also

affects seasonal changes in trees and shrubs used for landscaping. Deciduous trees and vines provide shade when it is needed in the summer but allow most of the sunlight to stream through their bare branches in the winter. Evergreens can be planted on the north and west sides of the house to block bitter winds as well as the hot sun of summer afternoons.

The next two chapters focus on the design issues that must be considered in planning homes that live with the sun. "Planning Floor Space and Site Orientation" presents issues related to the overall design of the home and its position on the property. "Building the Sun-Oriented Home" discusses design and construction details that improve any home's efficiency in using energy, no matter what the source.

Planning Floor Space and Site Orientation

A SUCCESSFUL HOME PLAN BALANCES THE PRACTICAL NEEDS OF THE OCCU-
pants, the unique attributes of the building site, and a clear sense of style. All
three factors are important. The practical needs — or, in architectural terms,
functional program — include general requirements for day-to-day activities
such as preparing meals, dining, sleeping, entertaining, playing, and working.
The daily routines and preferences of the occupants will influence the arrangement of spaces. For instance, a family may want a kitchen that is open to a family
room, or they may want a kitchen that is separate. They may want all the bedrooms clustered together, or they may want the children to sleep on a separate
level from the parents. They may also have particular needs, such as the desire
for a nook to curl up in and read, or for open cookbook shelves in the kitchen.

The building site also has an enormous impact on the livability of any
home. Location, access, views, landscaping, exposure to wind and sun, and
proximity to neighbors are some of the factors that must be considered in siting a
home and planning the interior spaces. Optimum exposure to the sun is
especially crucial for solar design. Other site characteristics such as the direction of slope, location of existing trees, and direction of access also play an
important role.

This chapter presents various criteria for planning interior spaces and
orienting your home on the building site. Your plan will probably not fulfill all
the criteria — few do. But the information will enable you to set priorities and
make informed decisions about your new home so you understand all the options
when trade-offs become necessary.

Inventory Your Family's Lifestyle

Every family has a variety of needs that must be met in the home — needs for sleeping, playing, dressing, storing clothes, preparing meals, eating, entertaining, watching TV, etc. We normally associate these functions with specific rooms, such as bedroom, dining room, or kitchen. However, at the early stages of home planning, it is useful to ignore traditional room designations. Instead, focus on the daily activities that will occur in your home and the way in which these activities use living space. Then you will begin to see relationships between spaces — the way activity in one area affects activity in another. For instance, noisy activities in one room make it difficult to carry on quiet activities, such as sleeping or studying, in an adjacent room. Play areas for toddlers should be located where adults can keep an eye on them. And a patio ideal for outdoor eating ought to be conveniently near the kitchen.

Besides thinking about the relationships between areas, you should also consider your space requirements for each activity, in terms of room size, storage needs, and type of access (single door, several doors, open entryway). Also consider any special features you want to include — perhaps natural lighting, access to a deck or terrace, a fireplace, built-in seating, soundproofing, or wall space for particular pieces of furniture or art. Finally, don't overlook the emotional and aesthetic impact you want from each space. This is an elusive, intangible consideration, but it is very important. As you imagine the perfect space for each activity, ask yourself such questions as: Do we want it to feel cozy and cavelike, or bright and open? Do we want the space to interact with the outdoors, or to focus inward? Do we want it to be stimulating or serene? Should it be formal or informal?

Of course, your choice of the finish details and furnishings has a great deal to do with creating the desired ambience of a room, and these choices can be made as the home is being completed. But the main architectural features, such as floor plan, ceiling height, and location of windows, also have impact, and they should be considered early as you go about selecting a plan.

The following checklist is an example of the kind of inventory you can develop of your family's needs for each type of living space. It will help you think of your home in terms of daily living patterns and not just as a collection of rooms. Then you will have a clear set of criteria for evaluating different home plans and selecting one that best fits your needs. Keep your inventory handy so you can update and revise it as fresh ideas come to mind. Don't forget to consider all the members of your household in this process — frequent visitors, youngsters away at school, even children who aren't born yet. And plan for the future, when your home may become an empty nest. If you are tempted to reject certain ideas because they seem to conflict with other needs, list them anyway. They may take on new importance if your priorities change, or you may see a creative solution to your conflict in one of the plans. Finally, make your list large and leave lots of space under each category. You may even want to use separate file folders for each type of space.

By clarifying your needs for each space and gaining a sense of how spaces relate to one another, you can begin to look discerningly at home plans to see if they are organized in the best possible way for your own family. You can evaluate them according to your daily living patterns, as well as for overall appeal. It may simplify the process if you group activities into broad categories, such as areas for public use (kitchen, dining room, family room, living room), areas for private use (bedrooms, study, bathrooms), and service areas (utility room, laundry). Study the arrangement of spaces within each area, and their relation to one another.

At this point it's also helpful to consider how you want each room and cluster of spaces to interact with the outdoors. Which rooms should capitalize on views? Which rooms need the most privacy? Which areas should have direct access to the outdoors? Which areas need to be quiet? These requirements will give you more guidelines for selecting a plan. Your choice will be influenced by issues of proportion and style and by conditions of the site, such as views, slope, access, privacy, landscaping features, and exposure to the sun. The more you are able to clarify the various issues, the easier it will be to choose the best plan for your lifestyle and your building site.

Inventory of My Family's Needs

Type of Space	Who Uses It	Activity	Next to or Near	Size of Space	Type of Light	Special Features	Ambience Desired
office	Mom	computer/ files	kitchen	8x10	north	view of play yard	efficient organized
bedroom	Dad/Mom	sleep/dress	office bath	16x20	morning sun	fireplace 2 closets	cheery/ like favorite bed & breakfast
retreat	Dad	read/relax	remote	10x12	any	double as guest room	dark
bedroom	Alex	sleep/study	bath patio quiet	12x12	south	quiet (late sleeper) view of trees	rustic
bedroom	Kate	sleep/study	play area	9x12	east	slumber parties	bright
gathering	all	watch TV/ eat informally play music	kitchen bath patio	20x20	south	fireplace storage wall	open, airy
cooking	Mom/Dad	store food prep/bake/ clean up	patio	14x16	east/south	good view breakfast nook	country
formal	all	entertain/ display/art	kitchen entry	20x24	south	fireplace	elegant
workroom	Dad	woodworking/ repairs	garage	20x20	north	large door	functional

Assess the Viability of Solar Heating in Your Region

As you sort through dozens of house plans, you must juggle a great many questions. How will this plan accommodate our sleeping needs? How will it work on our site? Does it suit our entertaining style? Where will the children play? Does the entry set the tone of formality or informality that we want? Is there enough room for overnight guests? Will the best views be showcased? Is there privacy from neighbors? Does the style blend with the neighborhood? What is the solar potential?

To answer some of these questions, you will need to examine the arrangement of interior space; for others, you must look at the interaction between indoor and outdoor spaces. But one of the first issues to investigate is the potential for solar heating, because it affects the orientation of the home on the site and, to some degree, the arrangement of interior space. With an understanding of basic solar principles and the solar conditions of your particular site, you'll be able to narrow your selection to those plans that, given your location, can use passive solar principles successfully.

Solar conditions vary by geographical region. Cloud cover, outside air temperatures, and the frequency of sunny days determine to what extent solar heating is possible in your area. Ideal solar conditions — lots of winter sunshine — are necessary only if you plan to depend on the sun for most of your heating. But if you are making only limited use of the sun for heating, lighting, and ambience, getting the overall solar picture is a good start for planning your home.

Solar homes have been built in many climates in recent years, and the results are very encouraging. Owners report that the homes are comfortable and beautiful and have low energy bills. Performance has generally depended more on energy conservation features — features that should be included in any home — than on techniques for tapping the sun's energy. Most problems have been due to excess: too much glass, too little or too much mass, too little shading, too much work operating movable window insulation, etc. By stressing energy efficiency in all homes and tempering the excesses of early solar

designs, architects have been very successful in incorporating solar principles into traditional home designs.

Local solar conditions help determine the optimal size of thermal mass, techniques for shading, and total window area for your home — and, of course, whether it's even possible for you to heat with the sun in the first place. The following guidelines give you a general idea of feasibility in your area, but consult local building authorities, a local solar or heating contractor, local architects, or the weather bureau about your specific region before making final decisions.

Colorado and some areas of the Southwest, where winters are harsh but sunny, are ideal for solar heating. Large window areas and lots of thermal mass are possible because of the abundance of sunshine. Other areas with harsh winters, such as northern New England, New York, and the upper Midwest, do not have as much winter sunlight and cannot depend on solar heat for as large a percentage of winter heating. Window areas and thermal mass should be sized accordingly, and insulation and energy-conserving features must be relied on more. Where summers are hot, east- and west-facing glass should be kept to a minimum. Where winters are less harsh but subject to cloudy conditions, such as the Pacific Northwest, direct solar heating is possible but should be limited to sunrooms with little or no thermal mass. More temperate regions, such as southern New England and the central coast area of California, require only modest passive solar systems along with standard energy-conserving features. In some regions cooling is more important than heating. Homes in the Gulf states, where humidity is a problem, require extensive shading and ventilation. This information may be useful to you as a general guide, but conditions in your local area and on your actual building site must also be considered.

Tracking the Sun

The first factor affecting solar design is the path of the sun throughout the day during each season. The sun swings an arc roughly from the eastern horizon to the western, reaching a certain altitude at midday depending on the time of year. In the northern hemisphere the highest altitude occurs at noon (solar time, which is approximately standard time) on June 21 (the summer solstice), when the sun is almost directly overhead. On December 21 (the winter solstice), the sun's arc is at its lowest, staying the closest to the southern horizon. The next day it begins to gain altitude again. This change in the sun's altitude as the seasons progress affects how the sun's rays strike the walls and windows of your home. In the winter the low sun penetrates south-facing windows during most of the day, but in the summer it is so high overhead that much less sunlight enters south-facing windows.

Not only does the sun change altitude during the year, it also rises and sets at different points on the compass. We think of the sun as rising in the east and setting in the west, but in the United States there are only two days out of the year when it actually rises due east and sets due west. Those days are March 21 and September 21, the spring and autumn equinoxes. During late spring, summer, and early fall, the sun rises progressively north of due east and sets progressively north of due west, so that north-facing windows actually receive direct sunlight. Conversely, in late fall, winter, and early spring, the sun rises and sets south of due east and due west.

Another factor that affects the sun's path, besides time of year, is geographic latitude. The farther south your home, the higher the sun swings its arc. The height of the sun at midday on December 21 is approximately 34 degrees above the horizon in our southern states and approximately 20 degrees at locations on our northern border. The points on the horizon where the sun rises and sets also vary with latitude. The farther north, the farther from due east the sun rises and the farther from due west it sets.

The practical impact of all these changes is important when planning the best site orientation, window placement, room arrangement, shading techniques, and location of solar collectors, if used. The sun will not shine into your windows in the same way throughout the year. South-facing windows will receive about twice as much solar radiation in the winter as they do in the summer. East- and west-facing windows will receive about two and one-half times as much sunshine in the summer as in the winter. In most cases these seasonal solar changes coincide nicely with seasonal weather changes. The sun shines into south-facing windows when it is needed most. Problems occur with east- and west-facing windows, which tend to receive

SUN PATHS ACCORDING TO SEASON

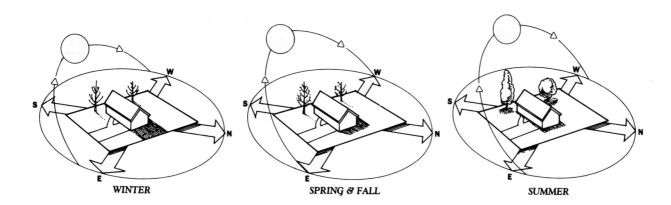

WINTER   SPRING & FALL   SUMMER

The path of the sun changes with the seasons. Not only does its altitude change, but it also rises and sets at different points of the compass depending on the season.

too much intense sunlight during warm months and not enough sunlight during the winter. However, by limiting window area, providing shade, and carefully planning the placement of rooms, many of these problems can be solved.

Calculating Heating Needs

Direct solar gain can provide a large share of winter heating, given proper orientation and good solar design. The exact amount can be estimated, based on how much solar energy is available and how much heat a particular home needs in your climate. If you are interested in this type of analysis, consult books listed in the Bibliography (page 185) or have a professional solar designer do it for you. The important thing is knowing what the sun is going to do at various times of the year, and how it will work with your plan.

Identify the Solar Resources of Your Site

Many site conditions affect the comfort, livability, and energy efficiency of a home. Those discussed here are especially crucial for homes that live with the sun. Conflicting needs and wishes are inevitable, so be prepared for compromises and trade-offs. Most of the windows should face south for solar gain, for instance, but if the best views are to the north, east, or west, you may have to make adjustments. Recording all your information onto a site map will make it easier to see the impact that different factors will have on your home and how those factors relate to one another. You will find instructions for making a site map of your property on pages 38 through 41.

Seasonal Amounts of Sunshine

Regional data will give you a good idea of how much solar radiation is available in your area, but you still need to assess how much is available to your actual building site. It is not necessary to visit the site throughout an entire year to observe sun angles and possible obstructions. You can use a solar viewer to get all the necessary information in one visit, even on an overcast day.

A solar viewer can be obtained from a solar equipment supplier or perhaps borrowed from a local architect or solar contractor. It is simply a curved piece of transparent plastic with lines drawn on it to represent the path of the sun at the summer and winter solstices (June 21 and December 21) and the equinoxes (March 21 and September 21). These lines are intersected by vertical lines that indicate various times of day, from early morning until late afternoon. The sun paths vary according to latitude, so make sure you have a viewer specified within 4 or 5 degrees of your latitude.

Stand where you plan to build, hold the device level, and aim it due south (not magnetic south). Look through it and you can trace the path of the sun against the actual horizon, noting the position of the sun at any hour of the day during any of the four seasons. You can see instantly how trees, hills, buildings, or similar obstructions will block the sun. The December 21 pathway is the most critical; the sun should be visible from 10 a.m. to 2 p.m. for solar heating to be feasible. You can repeat the same operation for any other time of the year. The site is ideal for solar exposure if, in sighting along the angle of altitude, you see no obstructions.

If there are obstructions, consider placing south-facing windows high enough for the sun to reach over them, or siting your home elsewhere on the property. Also keep in mind that although deciduous trees will be bare during the winter, they still can block a substantial amount of sunlight. Avoid a site that has too many deciduous trees on the south side of the house.

Views and Privacy

As you stand on the building site, note the views in all four directions, far and near. Use a compass to help you plot them on your site map and label them as pleasant or undesirable. Then try to imagine windows where they will take advantage of the most desirable views, and consider whether these windows will be

Continued on page 42

LOOKING THROUGH A SOLAR VIEWER

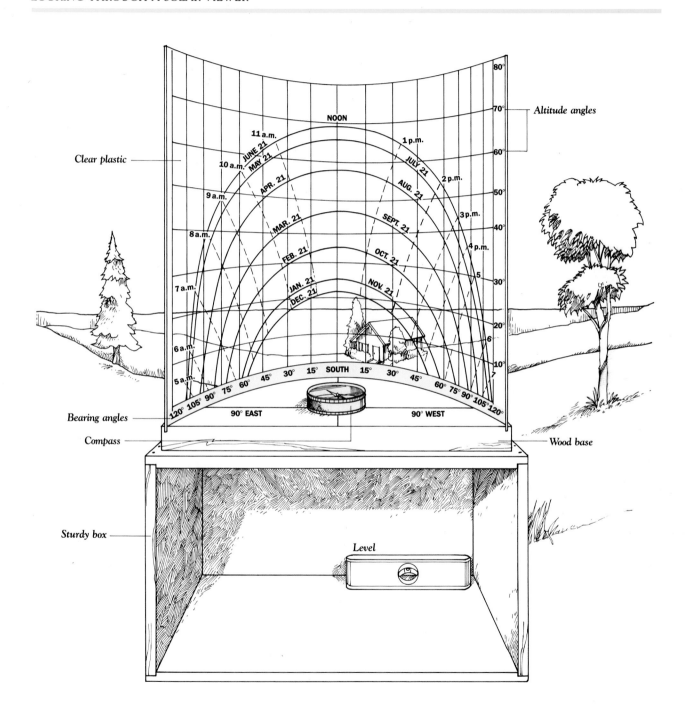

A solar viewer lets you see if there will be any obstructions that
might limit solar exposure.

DEVELOPING A SITE MAP

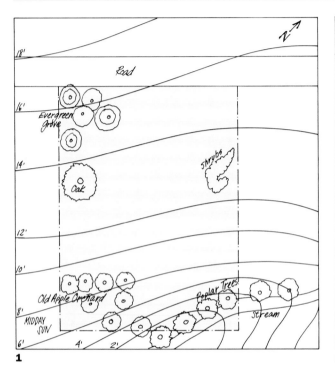

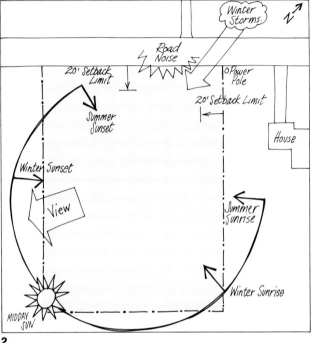

(1) To make a site map, start by plotting the property lines. Then add contour lines to indicate the approximate slope and natural features, such as ponds, trees, streams. Also indicate roads. If a survey has been done, you can get this information from the survey map. Otherwise, you can make some rough guesses until you need to have a survey made for other purposes, such as obtaining a building permit.

(2) Next, record as many features as possible onto your map. You may want to make separate maps and then consolidate all the information on one map when you get home. Note the location and approximate size of neighboring buildings, utility poles, street lights, and driveways. Indicate setback lines where applicable. You will need an assistant and a hundred-foot tape measure. Observe where noise comes from. Ask neighbors about prevailing winds and the direction of winter storms. You can also note the location of sunrises and sunsets, based on local solar data.

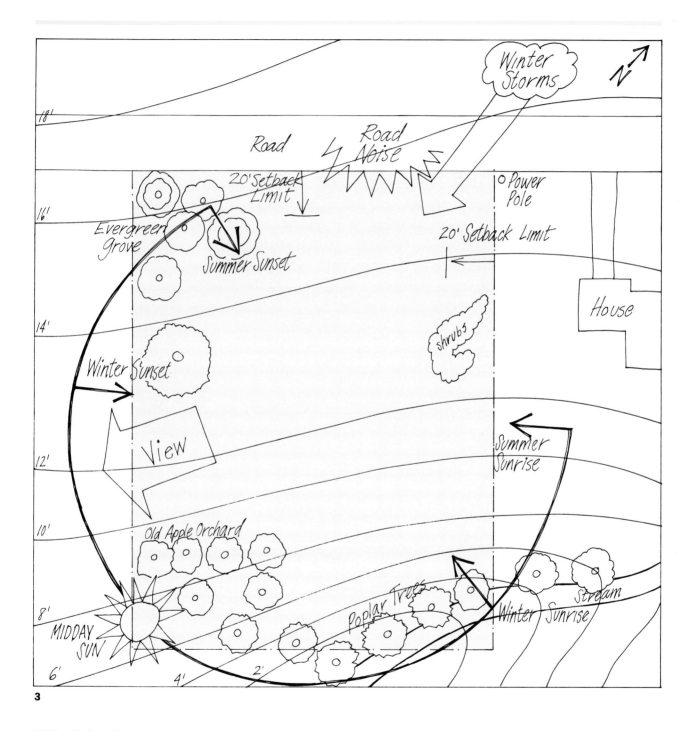

3

(3) Put all the information onto one map and make copies.

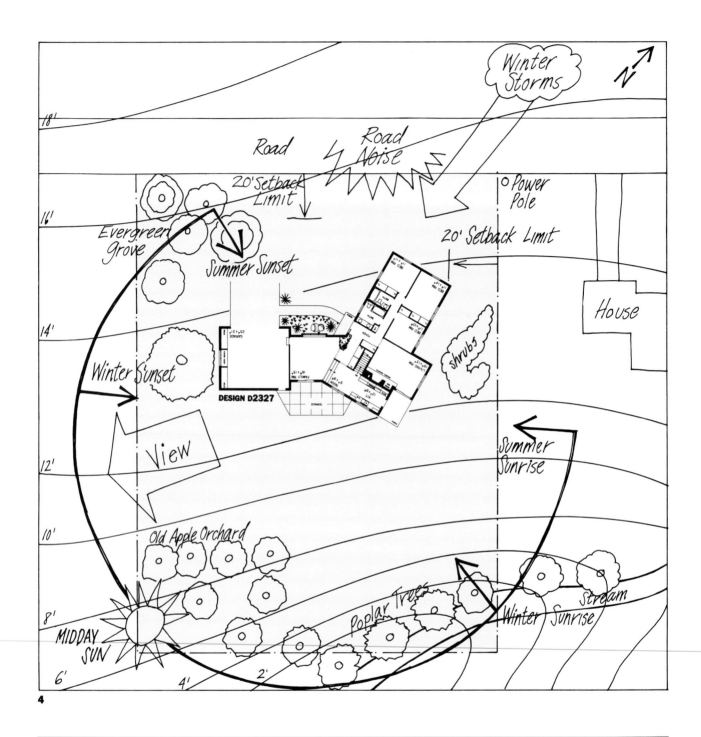

(4) Choosing a home plan you like, make an outline of it drawn to the same scale as your site map and experiment with various orientations and locations. In the example shown here, Design D2327 has been placed over the site map so that the garage door faces the road. The family room and the kitchen have the best views to the southwest. The garage and evergreen grove serve as a buffer against the hot afternoon sun of the summer and any winter storms from the west. Two of the bedrooms are close to the road, and two of the bedrooms have direct views to the neighboring house. The living room windows face a clump of shrubs instead of an open view.

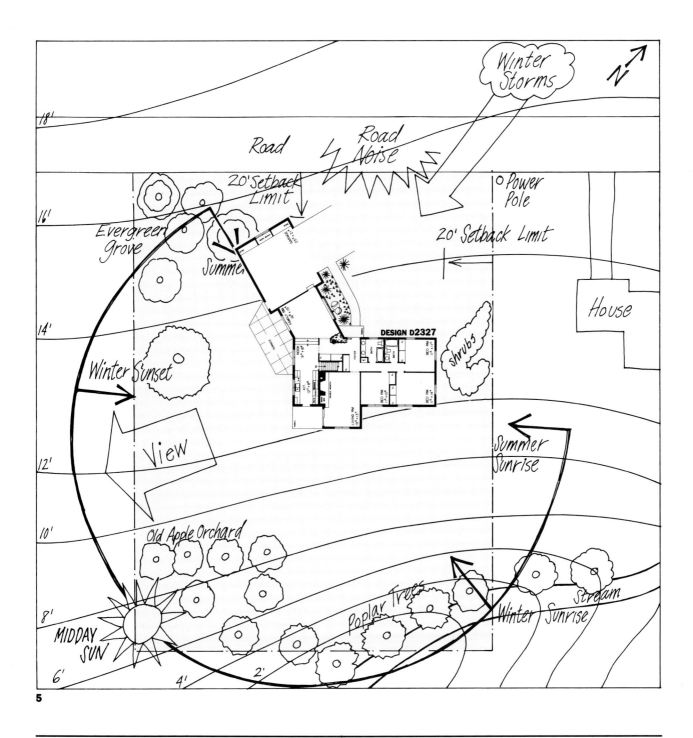

(5) Rotating the home solves many of the problems of the first siting and takes advantage of more of the natural landscape. The living room now has a window facing the most desirable view off to the southwest, and the view from the main window has been improved. Two of the bedrooms now look out on the open area behind the house instead of the neighbor's house. The bedrooms also are sheltered by the bushes and set back farther from the road than before. The kitchen and family room still have the advantage of the desirable view to the southwest, although they don't receive sun from the south as directly as before. However, the living room and two bedrooms re-ceive more daytime sunlight now. The garage serves as a better buffer against northwest storms and road noise than before, and the front entry is farther from the road and cre-ates more opportunity for a privacy garden.

screened from neighbors and passersby. Finally, see whether, in facing most of the windows south for solar gain, they will still have the best views. Again, you may have to consider other building sites in order to have windows with the best combination of views, privacy, and solar gain.

Land Contours

Which way does the ground slope? A site that slopes toward the south offers the greatest potential for solar gain. The downhill side of the house can have more than one level of south-facing rooms, and the north side can be nestled against the hillside for maximum weather protection. A level lot is also acceptable. But a site that slopes downward toward the north makes it difficult to orient the home toward the sun. Trees, nearby houses, and the hill itself may block the sun, and the best views and most likely window locations will probably face north.

Noise

Noise from highways, airports, and industrial zones can make a home unpleasant and should be considered in planning windows. If all the windows in the house are not double-glazed, at least those facing the source of noise should be. When possible, for the noisy side of the house, use fixed windows instead of windows that open. If the windows must be open for ventilation, arrange the rooms so that only those intended for active or infrequent use are exposed to the noise. Outdoor living spaces should also be shielded from excess noise, either by placing them on the opposite side of the house or protecting them with a solid wall or fence. Shrubs and hedges can also be effective sound baffles.

Breezes

Living spaces should be buffered from prevailing winter winds. If they come from the north, this can be done easily with dense landscaping on the north side, a low building profile on that side, and the placement of

garage, closets, utility rooms, and other incidental spaces on the north side.

Take advantage of prevailing summer breezes for cooling by placing windows opposite each other to create cross drafts and keeping vents low on the inlet side and high on the outlet side. Also place decks and other outdoor living spaces where they will benefit from gentle breezes.

Temperature Micropockets

Sometimes certain features of the terrain create temperature zones that differ from the surrounding area. A home nestled in the bottom of a gully may be subject to frosts sooner than other homes in the area, and a home perched on a west-facing slope may get unusually hot in the late summer afternoons. As a rule, cool air settles in gullies and swales or at the base of hillsides, creating colder conditions in the winter; strong winds can sweep down mountainsides; warm air rises up ridges and concentrates where breezes stagnate; fog often settles near lakes, rivers, or bays. Talk to neighbors to find out about local conditions and how they differ from the region as a whole.

Landscaping

Study your site to see if any existing trees or other landscaping features will provide shade or buffer winds and if there will be any problems planting new trees where needed. Look for evergreens to the north of the home site and deciduous trees that might shade the east and west sides. Foliage on the south side of the homesite should be outside a 45-degree arc to the south of solar windows. Trees or shrubs within this arc should be deciduous and should not have numerous branches that would block winter sunlight. Also, select trees carefully for planting. Some hold onto their leaves through December or January in certain areas. Large deciduous trees with limbs that would arch over the roof are desirable on the southwest and west sides of the home as well as wherever they would shield skylights. Use discretion in planning the removal of any trees. Certainly it would be acceptable to forfeit some solar gain to keep from sacrificing a magnificent hundred-year-old tree.

Use a solar viewer to gauge whether distant evergreen trees are too tall for winter solar exposure. For most latitudes, the winter sun will easily clear trees that are set back from the house a distance of twice their height.

Zoning and Design Restrictions

Cities and most counties enforce strict zoning regulations that govern the use and density of buildings. The regulations that pertain to standard residential dwellings, such as setback limits, regulations on auxiliary buildings, and lot-coverage ratios, also pertain to solar homes. However, there may also be design restrictions that apply to the overall architectural merits of a proposed home. These restrictions are more often implemented by neighborhood associations than by public agencies and would involve a design review process. Because they are concerned with external features such as site orientation, size and location of windows, shape of the house, pitch of the roof, and special details, they may prohibit certain solar features, such as roof-top

EFFECTS OF TREES

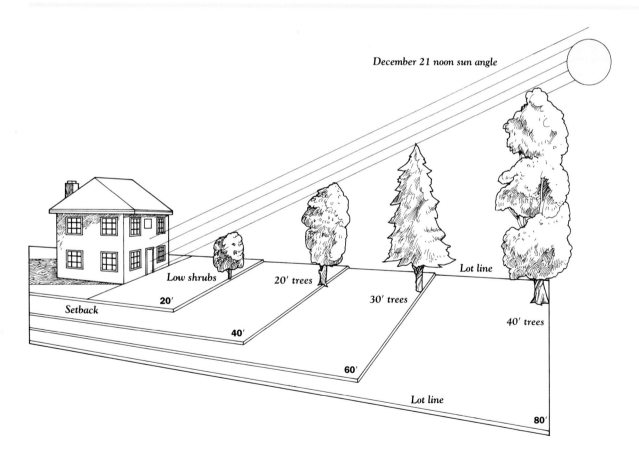

The south side of the house should be set back far enough from trees that they don't block the winter sun — unless they are deciduous trees without interfering branches.

collectors or massive glazing. You should be aware whether or not such restrictions exist in your community and be prepared to submit your plans for review if necessary.

Building codes, which are different from zoning and design restrictions, apply to the structural plans and construction details of your home. They are generally not considered in the site evaluation and preliminary planning stages of a project.

Orient Your House to the Sun

Because the sun's position changes throughout the day and seasons, the ideal home would rotate and tilt to correspond to its movements. A fantastically impractical idea, of course, and not even desirable—but it does emphasize the importance of a home's orientation for direct solar gain. Wall surfaces receive direct sunlight for relatively short periods of time, so they must be positioned to admit sunshine through windows or to block the sun at exactly the best time.

As much wall surface as possible should be oriented to the south for optimum heat gain in the winter. In the summer, these south-facing walls can be shaded with overhangs, trellises, and interior or exterior shades. Walls (especially those with windows) facing east and west should be as small as possible because they receive very little direct sunshine in winter but in the summer are exposed to low, intense sunlight for long periods. For these reasons the best home for solar exposure would have an elongated shape oriented along an east-west axis. A square shape is much less effective, and a home elongated from north to south is the least effective.

However, these principles are not absolute. For instance, if site conditions or functional requirements make it impossible to face the longest wall due south, it will still receive as much as 90 percent of the potential solar energy if it's oriented within 25 degrees of due

south (30 degrees in some latitudes). Sometimes it's preferable to orient the south wall slightly east of due south anyway, in order to catch the early morning sun for quicker heating. More heat is needed in the morning, when temperatures are cooler, than in the late afternoon.

A house that doesn't have an ideal rectangular shape can still be efficient under certain conditions. If it is on a south-facing slope, with a single story on the uphill side and several levels on the downhill side, it will have significantly more wall and window surface facing south than any other direction. A saltbox shape, with the roof extending closer to the ground on the north side, is another way of creating a favorable ratio of south-facing wall to north-facing wall. Super insulation (very thick wall and ceiling cavities that can contain much more insulation than normal), earth-berming (banking earth against some of the walls), and earth sheltering (placing earth against the walls and over the roof to increase insulation) are other techniques that can compensate for inefficient shapes. In extremely cold climates, a square shape can have an advantage because it is more compact than a rectangle, and thus conserves more heat.

The size and placement of windows are key factors in making the best use of the shape and orientation of a home. Building and energy codes limit the total area of window surface to a percentage of total floor area, usually between 15 and 20 percent. For best solar performance, a major share of this should face south—usually at least 40 percent of the total window area. In passive solar homes, south windows may equal as much as 10 to 20 percent of the total floor area. Window area on the north, east, and west walls should be held to a bare minimum by transferring some windows to the south side and reducing the size of those that remain. Just raising their sills will reduce the area of such windows without sacrificing desirable views, lighting, or ventilation.

The template on the next page, and the examples using actual house plans on pages 46 through 49, demonstrate how you can experiment with your favorite house plans to determine the optimal solar orientation on your site.

ORIENTING YOUR HOUSE TO THE SUN

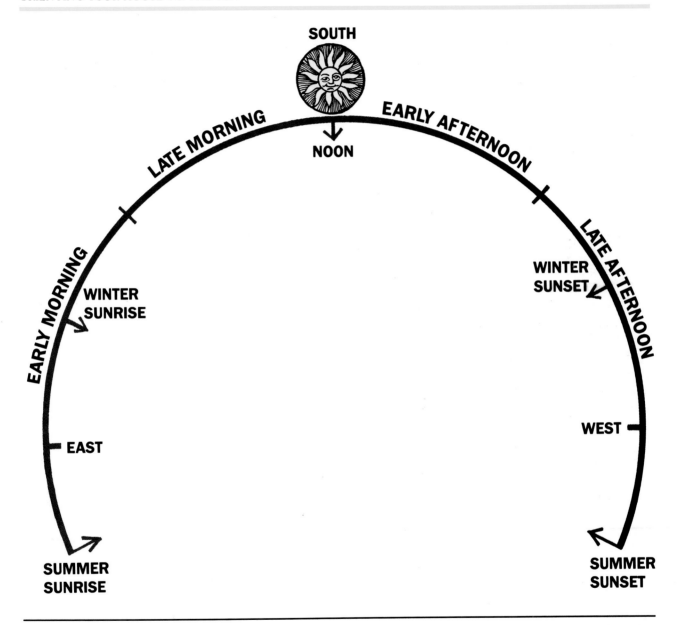

This template helps you visualize how a particular plan performs with different orientations to the sun. Simply make a copy of your favorite plan, cut out the floor diagram, and place it in the center of the circle. As you rotate it you can see how each window, room, and exterior wall will be affected by the sun throughout the day.

Keep in mind that the height of the sun above the horizon increases as it approaches the noon position. The arrows indicating sunrise and sunset are only approx-imations and will vary according to geographic region. The sun may also be blocked at certain times by hills, trees, buildings, etc., especially in early morning and late afternoon.

As you rotate the cutout plan, do not restrict the possi-ble positions to exactly north, south, east, or west. Skewing it slightly may provide a bet-ter orientation in some cases and may also align the house better with your lot lines, street, views, or other prom-inent features.

Continued on next page

DESIGN D2549

Front faces *east*. The morning sun shines into two bedrooms, breakfast room, and kitchen. The midday sun is blocked by the garage. The late afternoon sun shines into the dining room, living room, master bedroom, and downstairs rooms. The large windows on the back of the house all face west, causing overheating in summer and minimizing the potential for direct solar heating in the winter. There are no windows facing south for direct solar gain. The advantage of morning sun in the kitchen is outweighed by the disadvantages of this orientation.

Front faces *west*. The main window areas face east, causing potential overheating of these rooms in the summer and allowing very limited exposure to winter sunlight. Winter sun will not reach any rooms because of the absence of windows on the south wall. The west sun strikes two bedrooms and the breakfast room, causing overheating in summer evenings, in spite of some shading from the porch. This orientation has few advantages and many drawbacks.

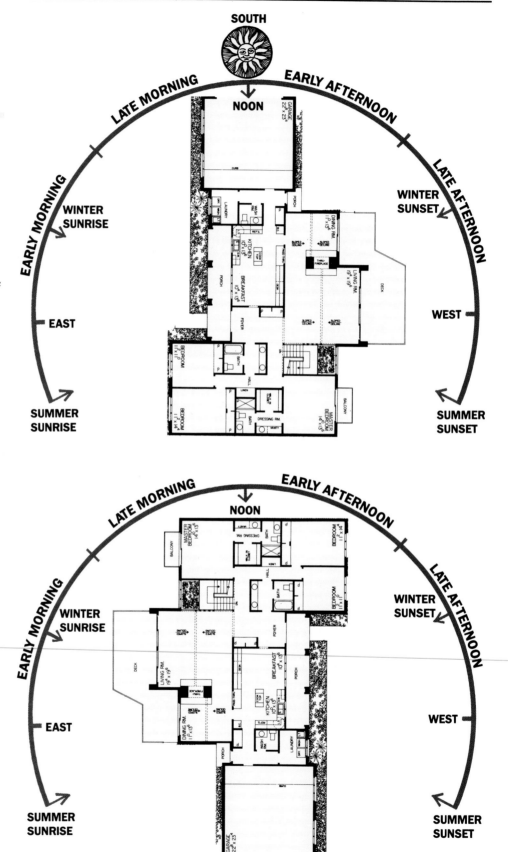

Front faces *south*. The main window areas are on the north side, where they will not receive the benefit of winter sunshine. The morning sun shines into only one bedroom and the daytime sun enters two bedrooms and the kitchen area during winter. This orientation makes poor use of the home's potential for solar heating and would be a net heat loser.

Front faces *north*. The main window areas face south for ideal solar exposure during the winter. The garage blocks the morning sun from the east, but other advantages offset this drawback. Only one bedroom is exposed to west sun. The kitchen and breakfast nook are on the north side and will not be subject to late afternoon overheating in hot weather. In this orientation, the elongated floorplan is aligned for the best energy efficiency. Rotating the front slightly toward the east will also work well.

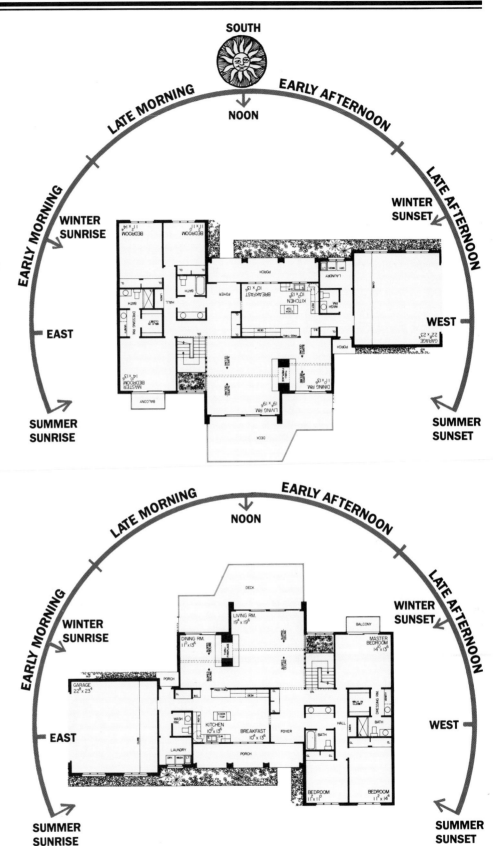

DESIGN D2823

Front faces *east*. The main window areas in the back of the house face west, causing problems with summer over-heating and eliminating the possibility of winter heat gain in the main living areas. Very few windows face south. The garage provides limited pro-tection from winter storms from the north. This orienta-tion allows very little winter solar heating and leads to sig-nificant heat loss through windows in the winter. In the summer the house would overheat excessively, both up-stairs and downstairs.

Front faces *west*. In this orientation the house has only two small windows fac-ing south: one upstairs and one downstairs. Most win-dows face east. Morning sun-light could quickly heat up the spaces, but by late morn-ing they would receive no more direct sunlight and be-gin to cool off rapidly. In the summer they would overheat by midmorning. The north side only has a window in the study, but this advantage is more than offset by the poor orientation of the main win-dow areas. The garage helps block the afternoon sun, but does not help to buffer the north side of the house.

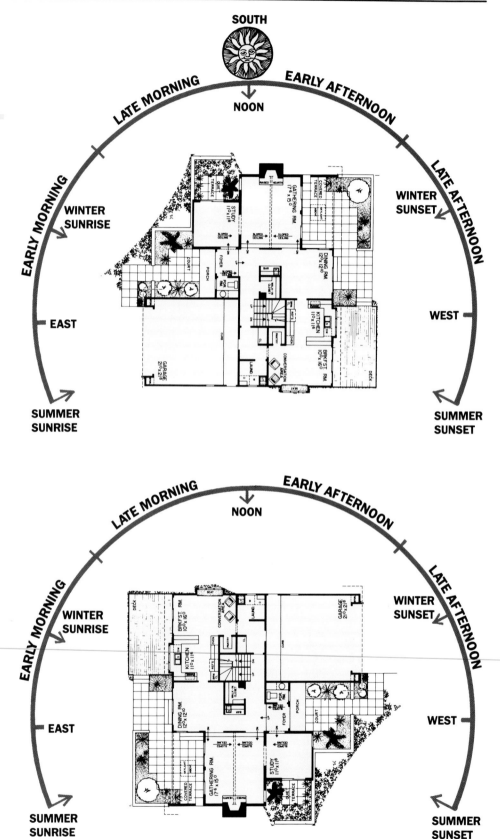

Front faces *south*. Two entire levels of windows face north and only three small window areas face south. The garage monopolizes valuable winter sunshine and only one bedroom receives any morning sunlight. The tall two-story wall on the back of the house bears the brunt of winter storms from the north. This orientation defeats every advantage of this gracious home for solar living.

Front faces *north*. The main window areas in the back face south for maximum solar heating. The roof overhangs and cantilevered upper floor help with summer shading. The garage provides a buffer against northern storms. The one-story front of the house provides further protection by creating a low profile with a long, sloping roof that would deflect winds. None of the bedrooms receives morning sun, although a small window could be added to the east wall of the master bedroom. The study receives early sunlight for morning use and indirect light the rest of the day. Exposure to the hot western sun is limited to a few small windows. The elongated shape of the home, without the garage, is oriented along an east-west axis for optimum southern exposure.

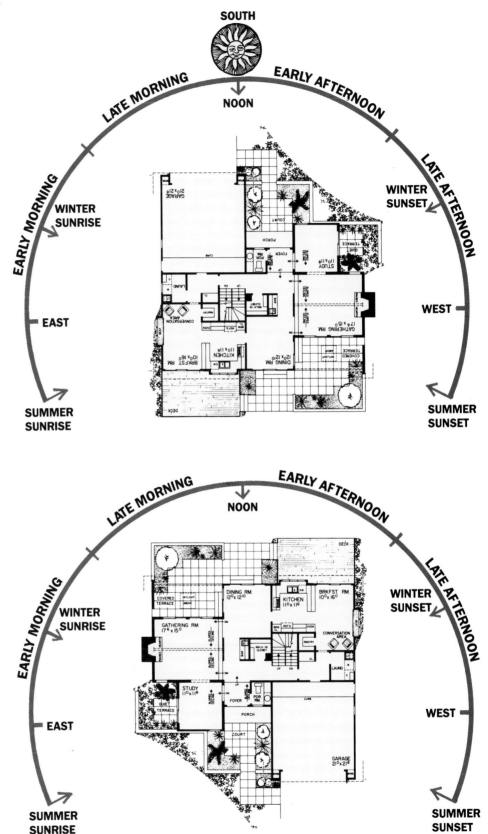

Organize Interior Spaces for Solar Living

Orientation and exterior shape are not the only elements to consider. The arrangement and size of the interior spaces are also important. Most people look at a floor plan in terms of living patterns and convenience, which are important, but the way in which the sun affects each room should also be considered.

Arrange Rooms to Capture the Sun

Interior spaces should be arranged to make the best use of the sun, but the final goal is not to create the most efficient solar home. It is to provide an environment that enhances the lives of those who inhabit it, an environment that is appealing, comfortable, and workable. Fortunately, bright interior spaces that admit direct sunlight at the proper times and shade it at other times add to the livability and aesthetic pleasure of almost any home. Notice how artists, over the centuries, have been fascinated by the effects of sunlight on interior spaces.

In general, the most frequently used rooms should be located on the south side of the house where they can benefit from daylight and direct solar heat during the winter months. Not every family would place the same rooms in this category, but the following are some possibilities.

KITCHEN.   The kitchen is the hub of activity in most homes, especially if it includes an eating or utility area. Most kitchens are occupied early in the morning, so they would benefit from east- as well as south-facing windows. Because cooking and utility use generate heat, kitchens are subject to overheating and should be protected from late afternoon sunlight.

NOOK.   An eating nook makes good use of south-facing windows. It makes a perfect place for breakfast on sunny mornings and for relaxing or reading on winter days — especially if it is large enough for a rocking chair or two, or perhaps a chaise longue.

FAMILY ROOM.   A family room that doubles as a play area for youngsters could benefit from sunlight during winter days, especially during after-school hours. It should have access to outdoor play areas.

DINING ROOM.   If the dining room is formal and is used only occasionally, it can be located on the north side of the house. A frequently used dining room, or one combined with family or living room areas, could be located along the south wall.

OFFICE.   If you spend a lot of daytime hours in a home office, you can take advantage of direct heating from the sun. It is especially welcome in the morning to get you in a working mood, so try to orient windows to the east as well as south. Avoid west windows if the afternoon sunshine makes you sleepy. Glare can be a problem in a working environment. Diffuse glazing spreads out direct sunlight and can minimize glare, but also distorts views. If glare might be a problem, place the actual working surfaces out of direct sunlight. Computer equipment should be protected from direct rays, as should any documents or books that might fade.

LIVING ROOM.   Even if a living room is not used much during the day, direct solar heat is still desirable. Heating such a large space with free sunshine will reduce the total heating load of the home, and floor and wall surfaces that bask in sunlight all day will likely be warm in the evening. Choose your furnishings and fabrics carefully lest they fade in all that sunlight.

BEDROOMS.   Place bedrooms that are used during the day for play, study, relaxation, or other activities along the south wall for direct solar gain. The sunlight will also benefit bedrooms by warming them for evening use. Choose an eastern exposure if you desire morning sunlight. During the winter, bedrooms with western exposures have the advantage of afternoon sun for studying or play, but in the summer overheating could make it difficult to put young children to bed early. Bedrooms used primarily for sleeping should be located on the north side of the house.

SUNSPACE. A sunspace should always be placed along a south wall for maximum heat gain, and it should open onto as many rooms as possible that are used during the day to help heat them. For this reason, a sunspace that is set back into the house is more effective for heating than one that protrudes from the house. If you desire a greenhouse with windows on three sides and skylights above, make sure it can be closed off from the rest of the house to prevent excessive heat loss during winter nights and minimize overheating in summer.

LUXURY BATH. Where privacy and space permit, you may want to place a luxury bath on the south side to take advantage of sunlight all day. An additional window on the east will enhance morning use. Usually, bathrooms are good candidates for the north side of the house.

The north side of the house should be reserved for rooms that do not require much window area. These rooms can help to buffer living spaces from bitter winds and cold outdoor temperatures during winter. Good choices are the garage, utility room, bathrooms, workshop, closets, stairs, hallways, entry, and storage area. Formal dining rooms and bedrooms used primarily for sleeping are other candidates.

Plan rooms carefully for east and west sides. Rooms with east-facing windows will receive morning sun, but in most climates these windows lose more heat than they gain in winter. They will usually provide heat only from late spring to early fall, so they should be minimized to avoid excessive heat loss in the winter and unwanted heat gain in the summer.

Likewise, west-facing windows will be exposed to hot afternoon sunshine in the summer and minimal heat gain in the winter. Therefore, rooms on the west side should have few if any west-facing windows. Orient them to the south or north instead. The primary exception is in areas with very cold winters and mild summers — use west-facing windows instead of north-facing windows. Garages, carports, and other buffers work well on the west.

These arrangements are all suggestions and not firm rules. They make the best use of light and heat from the sun but should be tempered by living requirements as well. If you have a spectacular view to the north or want to enjoy the sunset while you cook dinner, then put a living room on the north side with large windows or your kitchen on the west side, and make adjustments elsewhere for energy efficiency. The main goal is a home that creates the most pleasing overall living environment.

Integrate Spaces for Optimum Air Circulation

A home with large interior spaces that flow together is easier to heat and cool than a home with a number of small rooms. In the winter, warm air in one room quickly spreads to other rooms, and in the summer, cool breezes will flow more easily through the house. Open spaces also make rooms feel larger and bring family members together. However, a house still needs separate spaces where privacy can be ensured and where formal entertaining will not interfere with normal household life. Rooms that can be clustered together are the kitchen, breakfast nook, dining room, family room, living room, and hallways.

Another consideration, for multilevel and two-story homes, is convective air flow. Warm air rises and cool air descends, creating a circular flow. If a room that receives passive solar heating is lower than adjacent rooms, the warmed air will naturally circulate into them if a circular current can be maintained by the replacement of cool air.

It is difficult to find a perfect home plan that meets all your family's requirements, blends into the site, reflects the architectural flavor of the neighborhood, and works with the sun for maximum heating, cooling, and lighting. But the more familiar you are with your own requirements and the characteristics of your environment, the better prepared you will be to recognize a good and workable plan. And knowing how the sun affects living space gives you one more advantage in choosing the best plan for your family. The following three pages give examples of interior arrangements that work well with the sun.

ORGANIZING INTERIOR SPACES

DESIGN D2769

The rooms arrayed along the back of this home, which should face south, are the living room, dining room, nook, family room, study, and guest bedroom. The direct winter sunlight makes them all suitable spaces for daytime activities. The bedrooms on the east side stay cool. The master bedroom has a west window that admits afternoon sun.

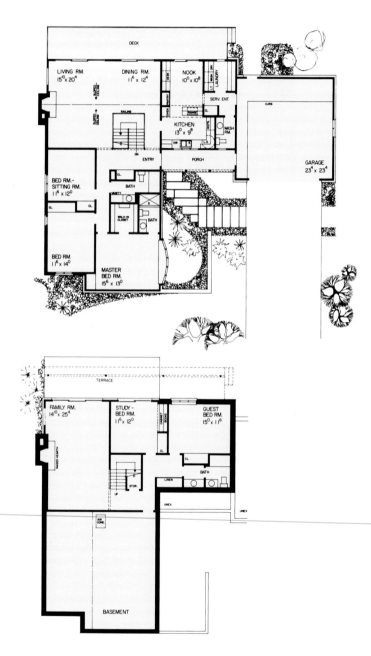

DESIGN D2692

When this home faces north, the study, kitchen, sunspace, clutter room, and two upstairs bedrooms receive direct sun during winter days. The living room and dining room are protected from the hot afternoon sun by their northern exposure and the garage. The bedrooms have a variety of orientations to suit all sleeping habits and preferences. This home is ideal when daytime activity revolves around the kitchen.

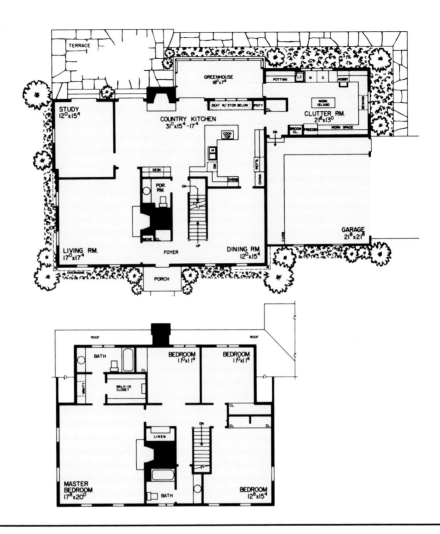

DESIGN D2905

When this home faces north, both upstairs and downstairs rooms receive direct sun during winter days, including the master bedroom, gathering room, dining room, breakfast room, and upstairs bedroom. The bathrooms, laundry, garage, entrance, and closets, all on the north side, are not affected by the small windows and lack of direct sunlight. The master bedroom has an east-facing window for morning sunlight, and the kitchen has a west-facing window that should be shaded to prevent overheating.

DESIGN D2921

When this home faces north, every room except the dining room and clutter room has south-facing windows for maximum solar exposure in the winter. Bathrooms, closets, entry hall, clutter room, and garage are located along the north wall. The kitchen receives morning sun and has direct access to the sunroom, which receives sunshine all day.

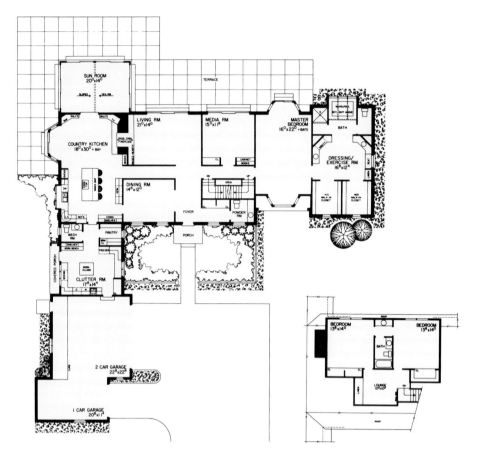

DESIGN D2863

Almost all the windows of this earth-sheltered home are along one side, which should face south. All the rooms, except the kitchen, are aligned along the south wall for maximum solar exposure. The north and west sides have no windows. The north wall accommodates the utilitarian spaces such as closets, bathrooms, laundry, and garage.

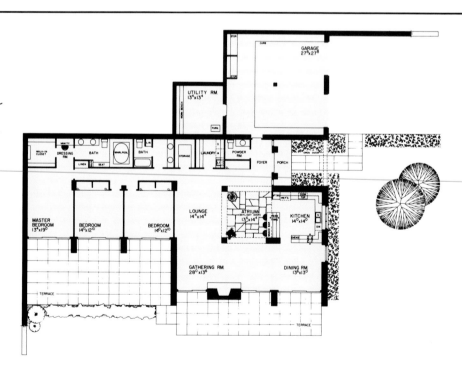

Building the Sun-Oriented Home

A HOME DESIGNED FOR LIVING WITH THE SUN MUST BE BUILT WITH ENERGY conservation in mind, just like any other home built today. Thanks to informed buyers, quality-conscious builders, and stricter codes, today's homes are tighter and more energy-efficient than ever before. The key to energy efficiency is attention to detail, from initial planning through the entire construction process. It's not just a matter of adding special features here and there, but of finding ways to save energy at every step of the project.

This chapter takes you through all the components of a home that relate to energy efficiency and solar gain. Not all of these features will be found in your working drawings; many are up to the discretion of the builder or homeowner. Some of these products and techniques are not widely known because they are basically regional practices or because they are so recently developed. But most are fairly easy to implement.

As you discuss your project with your builder, keep in mind that the goal is always comfort, not merely economy, and that you are building a home that should last a hundred years or more. Even if a miraculous new source of free energy were discovered tomorrow, many of the features described here would not become obsolete, but would still pay off in livability and comfort. These features are successful to the extent that they are integrated with timeless design principles and contribute to the comfort of the home's occupants.

Staying Comfortable

The range of indoor temperatures that humans find comfortable is very narrow compared to the extremes of outdoor weather conditions in most climates. One way to maintain the comfort range in your home is by constant conditioning of the indoor space with heaters and air conditioners, but this is a costly and wasteful solution. A better approach is to build into the home as many energy-saving and sun-oriented features as possible. The result is a home that accommodates the various positions of the sun — a "sun-tempered" home. It is not a collection of isolated components but an integrated whole in which the

COMFORT SENSATION

Air temperature
= 60°

Mean radiant
temperature of all
surfaces in room
= 78°

Comfort sensation
= 70°

We respond to a combination of air temperatures and surface temperatures (radiant) around us.
NOTE: *The temperatures shown here are for illustration purposes only, and not necessarily typical of all regions.*

building itself is a major part of the heating and cooling systems. To appreciate how these features work, it is useful to understand how a building affects human comfort.

We tend to think that the temperature of the indoor air is what makes us feel warm or chilly, but that's only part of it. We also respond to the tempera-ture of the objects and surfaces that surround us. All solid objects radiate heat outward to objects or bodies that are cooler. In homes, this radiant heat transfer, almost always unnoticed, has a substantial impact on our personal comfort. If the surrounding objects are cold, our bodies radiate heat toward them and we feel chilly. If they are warm, our bodies maintain a

RADIATING WARMTH TO THE COLD NIGHT

Outdoor temperature of sky = 20°

Surface of window = 50°

Body warmth

Air temperature = 75°

comfortable temperature, or sometimes even absorb unwanted heat from them. A good example is the effect of a skylight or picture window that is exposed to the clear night sky. Our body heat radiates toward it and makes us feel chillier than the air temperature would suggest.

Mean Radiant Temperature

The average temperature of all surrounding surfaces and bodies is called the mean radiant temperature (mrt). It combines with the temperature of the air to produce our overall sensation of being too cold, too hot, or just right. (Breezes, humidity, and concentrated heat sources also affect this sensation.) If the mean radiant temperature of all surfaces in a room is 80 degrees, the air temperature needs to be only 56 degrees for us to perceive it as a comfortable 70 degrees. Likewise, a high air temperature of 91 degrees is needed to overcome a mean radiant temperature of 55 degrees to make the room feel like 70 degrees. This chart shows the relationship between these two phenomena in creating our comfort sensation.

Mean Radiant Temperature	85	80	75	70	65	60	55
Air Temperature	49	56	64	70	77	84	91
Comfort Sensation	70	70	70	70	70	70	70

If the floors, walls, ceilings, furnishings, and other surfaces of the home are kept warm, the demand for heating the air can be greatly reduced during the winter. There are several ways to do this. The first requirement is to have adequate insulation, which helps surfaces stay warm by slowing heat loss through the building membrane — the exterior walls and ceiling, and the floor over an unheated space. The next step is to raise the temperature of the building's interior surfaces higher than that of the air around them. Radiant heating systems in floors and ceilings accomplish this; so do wood stoves and fireplaces, which heat objects

near them. Direct sunshine also heats objects and materials that it strikes for a sustained period. The heated surfaces in turn help to warm the air around them. The result is a constant, steady heat that is very comfortable.

The mean radiant temperature also affects summer cooling in the home. If surfaces are cool, our bodies radiate heat toward them and we feel cooler. However, if the surfaces are too warm, they make us feel even hotter.

Temperature Fluctuation

Another dimension of comfort is the extent to which indoor temperatures fluctuate. Individuals vary in their tolerance for temperature changes, but most are comfortable in the 10-degree range between 65 and 75 degrees. Outdoor temperatures, of course, fluctuate over a much broader range. Studies have demonstrated the relationship between indoor and outdoor temperatures in various types of unheated houses. In a poorly insulated home the temperature swings widely in quick response to changes in outdoor temperature. Such homes require constant indoor conditioning (heating or cooling) to maintain the temperature within the comfort range. As insulation is increased, the changes are not as pronounced, but can still vary by 20 degrees or more without some source of heat or cooling to balance the extremes. Buildings with the narrowest temperature swing are those with considerable thermal mass, usually in the form of concrete, stone, or brick. The dense material has a moderating effect because it is slow to absorb heat, store it, and release it back into the living space.

Using the building itself to help maintain steady, comfortable temperatures requires a proper balance of mass, glass, insulation, and back-up heating, achieved by paying close attention to every phase of the building project. The next two sections describe various components of a house and how they interrelate and contribute to comfort. The walls, roof, floor, windows, and doors comprise the exterior shell. This shell is like a large skin that encloses the interior spaces. As the first line of protection against the weather, it plays a major role in controlling heat loss, preventing overheating, and admitting desirable sunlight and fresh air. There are also important components inside the home — the interior systems — that are critical for heating, cooling, and ventilating. Taking care of each small detail, both exterior and interior, has a cumulative effect, making the entire house more energy-efficient and more comfortable.

The Exterior Shell

All components of the exterior shell are important, whether for structural reasons, aesthetics, livability, or energy efficiency. Those that have a critical role in solar performance are discussed in detail here, starting with the most dramatic and obvious: the windows.

OPTIMUM WINDOW AREA

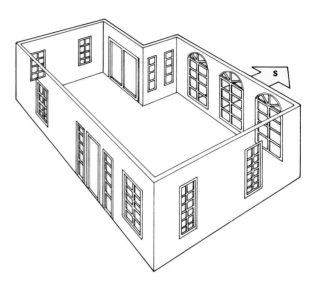

Total area of glass equals 15 to 20 percent of floor area. At least 40 percent of window area faces south for best solar gain.

Windows

Windows provide views, ventilation, and natural light. The average person spends 75 percent of the day indoors, so windows are important to health and personal well-being. They are also a key element in passive solar heating, along with proper orientation, thermal mass, low-energy cooling measures, and energy conservation features.

One of the critical steps in planning windows is calculating the proper amount of glass for a solar-efficient home. To provide daylight and ventilation, the total glass area for any home should be a minimum of 10 percent of the total floor area. For passive solar homes, windows should be designed to yield the highest possible net heat gain in the winter and the least possible heat gain in the summer. (Net heat gain is the total heat derived from sun shining directly through the windows less the total heat lost through windows at night and on cloudy days.) Too much glass causes problems with overheating and excessive heat loss at

night. Too little south-facing glass wastes an opportunity for free solar heat. Passive solar homes typically have south window areas equalling between 8 and 20 percent of the total floor area. These figures vary with climate and floor plan. If only a small portion of the home is being heated by the sun, the south-facing windows should be sized only for those rooms being heated, not for the entire home. As a general guideline, if the south window area exceeds about 8 percent of the total floor area, careful attention must be paid to sizing adequate thermal mass. One objective in the design of a passive solar home is to switch most of the glass that would be in the east, west, and north walls in a conventional home to the south wall.

Heat loss and unwanted heat gain through windows can be a problem in any home. However, there have been some promising developments in window technology, and you should consider them when you choose windows for your new home. Double-glazed windows are a bare minimum. They have two panes of glass held about half an inch apart and sealed around the edges to increase insulating capability. Such windows, using ordinary glass, have an insulating value of approximately R-2 — about twice that of a single-pane unit. However, R-2 is insignificant when compared with the surrounding wall insulation of R-13 or more. (The higher a material's R-value, or resistance to heat transfer, the greater its insulating ability.)

A major advancement in windows has occurred with the introduction of low-E (low emissivity) glass. A special coating on the glass blocks radiant heat from escaping from the living space, while allowing almost full sunlight to enter. A double-glazed window with low-E glass will have about the same insulating value as a triple-glazed window, but will admit more solar energy. In other developments, further insulation is achieved by replacing the air that is trapped between the panes with an inert gas such as argon, yielding a value of R-5 or more. Windows with an R-10 insulating value are now possible using a gel-like material instead of glass, and new developments may increase performance even more, so that the window area may be increased without risking heat loss.

The angle of the window also affects solar gain. Tilted windows, which seem to be aimed more accurately at the sun, are actually not as effective as normal vertical windows, are prone to leaks, and create an awkward profile. Vertical windows collect heat when it is needed most (i.e., when the sun is at a low winter angle) and also receive sunlight reflected from the ground.

Glare can be a problem with south-facing windows, but that can be controlled. Large windows and light color schemes create less glare, as do windows placed at roof level, such as clerestory windows. Daylight coming from a second direction, such as an east window or a skylight, also diminishes glare from a south window. In addition, avoid bright surfaces outside a window, such as concrete paving or parked cars, which can intensify glare. To control fading, use colorfast fabrics or light-colored furnishings. Windows coated with tin-oxide compounds can deflect most of the ultraviolet radiation that causes fading; however, they reduce the amount of passive solar heating.

Choosing windows for your home is an important part of planning. Besides glazing options, you will have many choices of format and frame style. These choices are primarily aesthetic, but energy conservation should also be considered. Wood frames, either painted or clad with vinyl or aluminum, offer somewhat better insulation capability than do aluminum frames. However, they do require maintenance, especially those without exterior cladding. Aluminum and other metal frames come in a variety of colors. Heat loss through the frame can be controlled somewhat by thermal breaks — layers of insulating material sandwiched between the metal pieces. Another important energy concern is air leaks around windows that open. Double-hung, casement, hopper, and awning windows should fit tightly and have weatherstripping. The best weatherstripping system consists of two or three rows of material instead of just one. Ask for the air leakage rating of a window. It should be less than .30 cfm (cubic feet per minute) per foot of sash length.

Energy conservation is a very important dimension in selecting and planning windows, but their architectural impact must not be overlooked. The placement, size, and style of windows affect the quality of indoor living in many ways. Pleasing views enhance the lighting and heating potential of windows, and create strong focal points. The size and lines of a window can make it an important architectural element that adds interest to any room. Windows placed high on a wall where they open to the sky have an uplifting effect, and tall windows at a corner lengthen the walls and enlarge the room. Trim details and window coverings create a finished, traditional look, and large fixed windows emphasize the outdoors. On the outside of the house, windows create rhythms and shapes that contribute to the style and unified feeling of the structure.

Insulation

Insulation and infiltration-control materials are among the least expensive materials in a new home, but the most important in saving money over the life of the house. Insulation provides a thermal barrier to minimize the flow of heat out of the house in cold weather and into the house in hot weather. The other materials, such as weatherstripping and caulking, reduce air infiltration, which accounts for a large percentage of heat loss during the winter. Recommended amounts of insulation differ according to climate. Local building or energy codes will specify how much to use for the floor, ceiling, walls, and foundation. Keep in mind that code requirements are for minimum amounts. Adding 20 to 50 percent more will usually increase your long-term savings. Beyond that, the payback benefit depends on local conditions.

SAMPLE INSULATION REQUIREMENTS

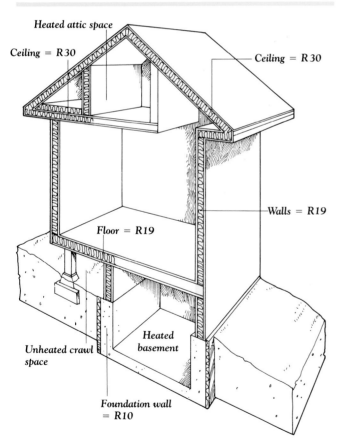

Heated attic space

Ceiling = R 30

Ceiling = R 30

Walls = R19

Floor = R19

Heated basement

Unheated crawl space

Foundation wall = R 10

NOTE: *This is a generic sample, not specific to any particular region. Consult your own building department for local requirements.*

How your insulation is installed is as important as how much is installed. It pays to be familiar with proper insulating techniques as you inspect the work. The most common type for new homes is fiberglass blanket insulation. Because it is flexible and light, it is easy to take short cuts in installing it. But gaps can destroy a home's energy performance. Batts should be cut to fit into stud cavities and joist bays perfectly, without being compressed or leaving gaps. They should be fitted carefully around obstructions such as electrical boxes, blocking, and pipes. Cracks and crevices should be insulated with small scraps cut to size, not compressed. Spray foam sealant, a urethane foam that comes in a can, may be used to seal and insulate tight areas. However, it should not be used around pre-hung window units because the expanding foam has a tendency to force the jambs against the window sashes so they will not operate correctly. (See the Bibliography on page 185 for more detailed information on insulation methods.)

In areas where outdoor temperatures frequently fall below freezing, a vapor barrier consisting of plastic sheeting should be applied on the interior side of insulated walls and ceilings. The barrier prevents moisture vapor inside the house from condensing within the wall. Accumulated moisture in the walls or attic will eventually cause rot. A properly installed vapor barrier should have overlapped and taped joints, and be sealed to all penetrations through the wall and ceiling, such as electrical boxes. In fact, an airtight wall or ceiling is the most important element in moisture control. An alternative to plastic sheeting, called the "airtight drywall approach," is becoming more popular in some regions. It requires that the drywall be sealed carefully to all wall penetrations.

Another type of barrier, called a "house wrap," is often applied to the outside of the walls before the siding is installed. It keeps drafts, dust, and insects from squeezing through tiny wall openings, but allows water vapor to escape. It is important that all joints are overlapped and taped. Other measures for preventing air infiltration include caulking all exterior cracks and joints; sealing holes where pipes, ducts, and wires penetrate floors and ceilings into unheated space; weatherstripping all doors and operable windows, including basement doors and attic hatches; applying caulk or insulation between foundation and sill plate; caulking between the subfloor and sole plate of framed walls; using stove cement to seal the gap around chimneys and flues where they penetrate the ceiling into an unheated attic or chase; making sure bathroom and kitchen fans have dampers; and placing a gasket over electrical boxes in exterior walls before installing the cover plates.

Each of these details may seem insignificant by itself, but they have a cumulative effect that makes the whole much greater than the sum of the parts. They are easy to overlook as the momentum of completing the job begins to take over, but most of them are

PREVENTING AIR INFILTRATION

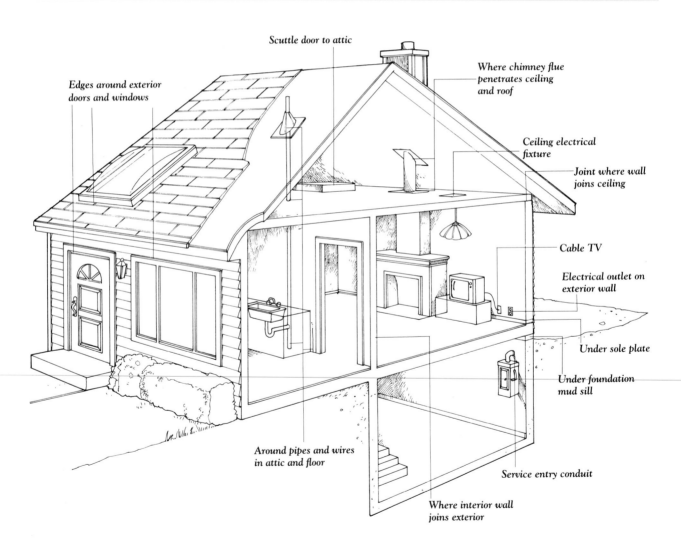

Scuttle door to attic

Where chimney flue penetrates ceiling and roof

Edges around exterior doors and windows

Ceiling electrical fixture

Joint where wall joins ceiling

Cable TV

Electrical outlet on exterior wall

Under sole plate

Under foundation mud sill

Around pipes and wires in attic and floor

Service entry conduit

Where interior wall joins exterior

Use caulking, weatherstripping, or foam to seal places where air might infiltrate.

impossible to do after the house is finished. A few extra steps at this point of construction will have enormous pay-offs in comfort and energy savings for a long time.

Thermal Mass

The amount of mass in a home has an important effect on comfort and temperature stability, especially in homes that depend on passive solar heating for most of their heating. All buildings have a certain amount of mass. Wood-framed houses have light floors and walls, so extra thermal mass is often added to wood-framed passive solar homes to absorb solar heat, store it, and release it back into the living space when needed. Concrete floors covered with brick or tile, massive masonry walls, or storage containers filled with water are the earmarks of such homes.

In homes where passive solar designs are intended to meet a major share of the heating needs, careful attention must be paid to providing sufficient thermal mass. Homes without much thermal mass should not have excessive window area. The most appropriate climates for high mass homes with vast areas of south windows are those with cold, sunny winters, such as the mountain and plateau regions of the West. Thermal mass also helps keep homes cool in the summer by absorbing excess heat during the day and releasing it at night.

In milder climates, especially those with relatively cloudy winters, the most practical approach is to balance a moderate amount of thermal mass with a moderate amount of south-facing glass (8 to 10 percent of the floor area). Some examples of moderate mass include a conventional four-inch-thick concrete slab floor, a masonry fireplace, a tile floor set in a mortar bed over a wood-framed floor system, a veneer wall of masonry behind a wood stove, and a layer of plaster over half-inch drywall. The mass is most effective where the sunshine falls directly on it.

A local solar designer can advise you on the best approach for your region. If extra thermal mass will benefit your home, it is fairly easy to incorporate into the basic structure. Masonry materials, such as concrete, tile, brick, and stone, can add mass, and beauty

as well. Other materials, such as water in storage containers and special phase-change materials in small containers, are more effective than masonry; however, they have other drawbacks. Water containers are not as compatible with home design as are masonry materials, and they can be difficult to integrate into an attractive arrangement. Phase-change materials (heat-storing chemical substances) can be built into a wall, but they are expensive and in most cases are not yet cost-effective. Whatever mass is used, it must be inside the insulated shell of the home, and as close to south-facing windows as possible.

Shading Systems

Shading keeps windows from letting in unwanted sunshine during hot weather. South-facing windows can be protected fairly well with fixed shading, such as roof overhangs or second-floor balconies. The overhang should extend far enough to shade the window completely during hot weather, but not so far as to block the sun when solar heating is desired. The actual size of the overhang depends on geographic latitude, the height of the window, and the month when shading is needed most.

The sun reaches the highest point of its annual cycle on June 21, but hotter weather usually occurs throughout July and August. However, if the length of overhang is based on the sun's position on August 21, it will also block the sun on April 21, when it may be needed. A good compromise is to size the overhang for shading on August 10, which has the same solar angle as May 3. The overhang would then extend a distance of one-quarter to one-half the height of the window, depending on latitude, and would be located above the window at a distance of eight inches for every foot of overhang. Consult a local solar designer for exact calculations.

If weather in your area tends to be erratic during late spring and late summer, adjustable shading devices, such as awnings or louvers, may be preferable. Another solution is to plant deciduous trees, shrubs, and vines, which produce leaves at times that tend to correspond closely to shading needs. However, the branches of deciduous trees can block considerable sunlight. Also, in many climates a few species of deciduous trees do not lose their leaves until December or even January. In the best landscaping plans, deciduous trees are planted on the southeast and southwest corners of the home, not directly in front of south-facing windows.

Fixed overhangs are not useful for windows facing east and west because the sun is so low during the hot summer months. Shrubs and low trees work better, although they may block desirable views. A wide trellis or awning may work if it extends far enough out from the house. Fixed vertical shading, such as fences and exterior shade walls, can sometimes be integrated into the home's architecture, but they may also block views and can create dark indoor spaces during winter months. Roll-up shade curtains work very well, but it is preferable to locate them outside rather than inside windows to prevent heat build-up. Interior shades should have a reflective or glossy white finish toward the outside. They should also be loose enough to allow air circulation behind them. Heat-reflective glazing or glazing films are shading options that preserve views from east and west windows, but should not be used on south windows because they would block desirable solar gain in the winter.

If you are fortunate enough to have large trees on your building site, they can shade the entire house with an overhead canopy of branches during hot summer months. The larger the tree, the less likely that branches will interfere with views at ground level. If there are not enough trees to surround the home, try to site it so they are along the southeast, east, southwest, and west sides.

SIZING A FIXED OVERHANG

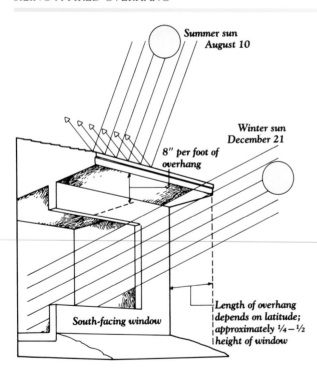

Summer sun
August 10

Winter sun
December 21

8" per foot of
overhang

*Length of overhang
depends on latitude;
approximately ¼ – ½
height of window*

South-facing window

NOTE: *If an overhang is more than one quarter of the full height of the window, it can be very expensive to construct. Consider using shades instead.*

Skylights

Skylights have dramatic appeal. They flood a room with daylight and offer nighttime views of the stars and moon. But they can also cause overheating and heat loss. Although not quite a hole in the roof, a skylight with dual glazing has an insulating value of only about R-2, whereas insulation in the surrounding ceiling would be R-30 or more. Far more heat escapes through this thin patch in the thermal blanket than through vertical windows of comparable size. Furthermore, the angle of tilt of a skylight is too flat to receive helpful winter sunshine, but just right for admitting the intense rays of the summer sun.

However, these problems can be controlled through shading and insulating systems. The best shading technique is to block unwanted sunlight before it can pass through the glazing. A shade on the inside must have a very reflective outside face or it will allow the sun to heat air next to the glass excessively; this air can then escape into the room. Outdoor shading, such as that provided by trees and accessory shades built into

SHADING TECHNIQUES

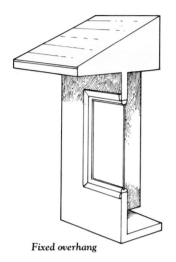

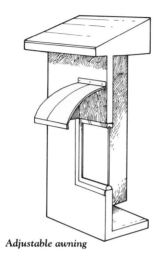

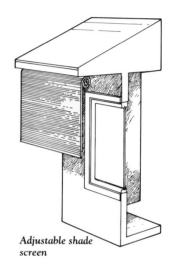

Fixed overhang

Adjustable awning

*Adjustable shade
screen*

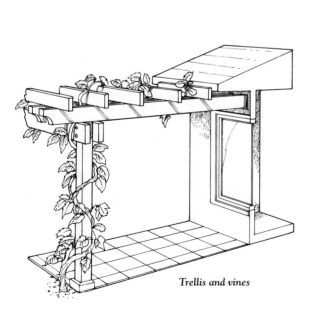

Trellis and vines

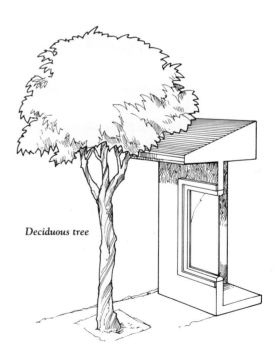

Deciduous tree

the skylight by the manufacturer, is much more effective in preventing heat build-up. In addition, opaque or bronze-tinted glazing reduces heat gain, although this may not be desirable year-round. Insulating quilts and solid insulating shutters improvised for a skylight provide insulation as well as shading. Solid shutters using foam insulation cannot have the foam exposed directly to the living space; it would be a fire hazard and would require one-half-inch drywall or equivalent protection. Automated louvers have been developed that provide insulation and shading at the same time. Most of these devices require the owner to operate them directly. Sometimes, the only option is to accept the loss in energy efficiency to have the pleasure that skylights can provide.

Ventilation

Fresh air for the living space is essential for health. Ventilation can bring in fresh air and improve air quality. Ventilation systems range from simple, inexpensive designs that use kitchen and bathroom exhaust fans to sophisticated centralized designs that require ducts run through the house.

Ventilation is also important for summer cooling. Operable windows and vents can be placed to capture natural breezes — they should be opposite each other and at different levels, if possible. Because natural breezes are never totally reliable, ceiling fans or a whole-house fan, which is located in the ceiling of a central hallway and draws air into the attic, will aid ventilation. While fans do not always lower the interior air temperature, they make people feel more comfortable at higher temperatures and reduce the need for air conditioning.

The crawl spaces under the house and the attic should also be ventilated to prevent the accumulation of moisture that could damage structural members. In crawl spaces, vents should be placed in corners for cross breezes. In addition, a plastic vapor barrier should be placed on the earth floor; this will cut moisture accumulation by over 90 percent. In attics, the best ventila-

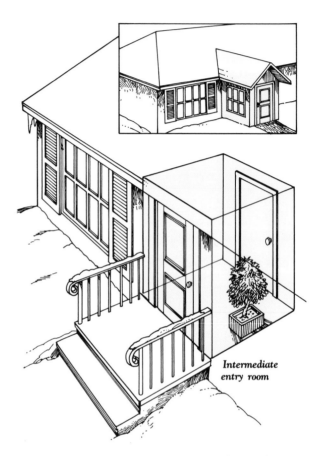

Intermediate entry room

An intermediate entry room keeps cold outdoor air from entering living space.

tion combination is a ridge vent running along the ridge of the roof and an uninterrupted soffit vent running underneath the eave.

Doors and Entries

Exterior doors should not be overlooked in making a home more energy-efficient. Every time a door is opened cold air is admitted, and even when they are closed most doors are not very good insulators. Insulated doors with higher R-values are available, however, and weatherstripping should be applied to all exterior doors. For areas with cold winters, an air-lock entry reduces cold-air infiltration. An air lock is a small transition room with a door to the outside and another door to the rest of the house, which makes it possible to enter and exit without exposing the living space to direct contact with the outdoors. Another good transition is entry through a sunspace. It provides a warm oasis on cold days and an inviting entrance into your home.

Efficient Mechanical Systems

he mechanical systems that provide heating, cooling, hot water, and conveniences comprise a large part of the initial construction budget. But because they have an even greater impact on month-to-month operating costs throughout the life of your home, they should be designed very carefully.

Heating Systems

Most homes need some kind of heating system, even if it's just an auxiliary heater for a predominantly solar-heated home. In bygone years, builders used simplified rules of thumb to size units and usually ended up with a substantially oversized unit. Now, most owners look at the lifetime operating costs of a heating system and want the most energy-efficient available. There are many choices to consider: the mode of heating (forced air vs. radiant, central vs. decentralized), type of fuel (natural gas, electricity, oil, wood, coal, solar energy), and energy-efficiency rating. The system must also be sized, taking into account the size and insulating value of each component of the building membrane, as well as the local climate, in particular the heating design temperature (the temperature that the heating system and building insulation are designed to maintain).

A central forced-air system is the most common mode of heating. It heats the home quickly, is operated by a central control, and can be combined with central air conditioning. Because it is so common, the installation and equipment costs tend to be competitive. For most regions, the most economical source of energy is natural gas. However, in warmer climates, electric heat pumps are being heavily marketed. In other regions, fuel oil is the most available and economical fuel.

Older heating systems were inefficient, but newer, high-efficiency furnaces can use over 90 percent of the heat potentially available from the fuel. So much of the heat is captured that the flue gases can be vented through plastic pipe. However, forced-air systems are not always the most comfortable form of heating. The warm air tends to rise toward the ceiling, while the mean radiant temperature of surrounding materials may remain cool. Noise can be another problem, as is the potential for recirculating unwanted pollens and pollutants. Another disadvantage is that the entire system is either on or off, although registers can be adjusted to regulate the amount of heat for individual rooms.

Radiant heating is quieter and more comfortable than forced air. One type uses electric resistance wires embedded in the ceiling or walls. It is very expensive to operate. Another type makes use of hot water pumped through pipes embedded in the floor. Older systems used copper pipes, which tend to corrode and leak. Newer systems using polybutylene or other plastic piping are much more reliable; the pipes resist corrosion, are more flexible, and come in rolls long enough so that few, if any, joints are necessary. The hot-water radiant system can use any heat source, such as a conventional gas furnace or a standard water heater. It is particularly suitable for active solar heating because it can be run at much lower temperatures than can space-heating systems (around 90 to 100 degrees). Because radiant heating produces comfortable temperatures without heating the air, it can be more efficient and economical to operate than other types. It can be installed in concrete slabs or under wood floors, and zoned so that only certain rooms are heated at certain times. The problem of slow heat build-up can be solved with a programmable thermostat, which can be programmed to start the system at certain set times instead of every time the temperature reaches a certain point. However, radiant systems are often more expensive than forced-air systems and may be difficult to service and repair. In warmer climates, radiant heating systems may overheat the house during weather with cool nights and warm days.

Baseboard systems, using convectors heated by circulating hot water or electric resistance elements, heat the air around the perimeter of a room and provide a source of radiant heat as well. The electric systems are more expensive to operate. The hot water systems, called hydronic systems, are quiet, don't cause drafts, and can be zoned to heat only certain rooms at certain times. Care must be taken to be sure the heat is not blocked by curtains, drapes, and furniture. Baseboard systems are reliable and simple, although the heat may not be as even and comfortable as that from radiant floors. However, like radiant systems, they can be expensive to install.

Wood stoves and fireplaces are popular options for auxiliary heating. They create a homey ambience and give off direct radiant heat. Problems with air pollution have generally been solved with catalytic combustors and other devices. High-efficiency wood burners coax every available Btu out of the wood, and attractive designs are available for almost any interior style. Fireplaces are again being designed for greater efficiency, borrowing from the classic Rumford design with its high and shallow firebox, or from Russian and Finnish designs with a massive masonry core. Glass fronts and ducts for drawing combustion air from outdoors also increase efficiency. Wood stoves and fireplaces require lots of attention, especially when they are used as a main heat source. The rituals of hauling firewood, building fires, cleaning out ashes, and sweeping the chimney are not for everybody. Wood is not necessarily a cheap fuel, and is not always readily available. Be sure to check with your local building department about any restrictions pertaining to the installation of wood-burning devices.

No matter what type of heating system you choose, energy efficiency depends on careful installation. All ducts and pipes should be insulated and sealed against leaks. Runs should be kept as short as possible, and flues should be located where any residual heat will benefit the interior living space. In some areas, flues should also have stack dampers to prevent cold downdrafts. Thermostats should be programmable to minimize heating when it's not needed. The system should be carefully zoned, with independent controls if possible, so that heat is delivered where it's needed. This is especially important for homes oriented to the sun, where some rooms will be heated by direct sunlight but others must rely on conventional heating.

Cooling Systems

Cooling should not be thought of as a mechanical system added to the home, but as a series of strategies to make the home comfortable as naturally as possible. For a home in tune with the sun, many of the techniques for cooling are compatible with those for heating. Even when air conditioning is required, natural cooling strategies will help to reduce the load and cut costs. The most important are shading and ventilation.

The first goal of cooling is to reduce heat gain from the sun. The shape and orientation of the building can be helpful in this. An elongated structure oriented along an east-west axis works equally well for cooling and heating. The amount of building surface exposed to the strong east and west sunlight is restricted and most of the living space can be aligned along the easily shaded south side. In extremely hot climates, the main living spaces should be clustered along the north and east sides.

Shade is also important for cooling. Windows should be shaded from direct sunlight by awnings, shade screens, trellises, vines, trees, or roof overhangs. The roof should also be shaded as much as possible by tall trees and plants. Large trees on the southwest and west sides are effective. The closer they are to the house, the less they will interfere with views.

Another way to reduce heat gain from the sun is with a radiant barrier installed inside the attic. This kind of barrier consists of a reflective membrane, much like thick aluminum foil, that is stapled up against the rafters. By reflecting radiant heat toward the sun, it

COOLING TECHNIQUES

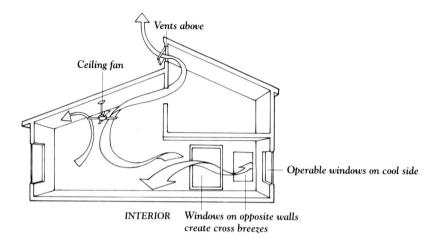

Vents above

Ceiling fan

Operable windows on cool side

INTERIOR   Windows on opposite walls
create cross breezes

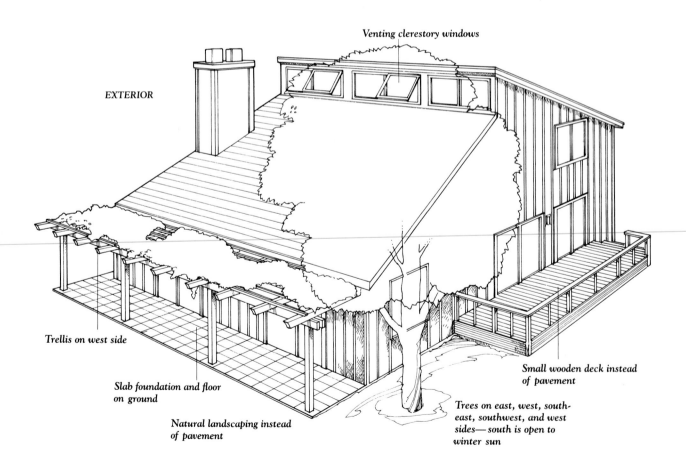

Venting clerestory windows

EXTERIOR

Trellis on west side

Slab foundation and floor
on ground

Natural landscaping instead
of pavement

Small wooden deck instead
of pavement

Trees on east, west, southeast, southwest, and west
sides— south is open to
winter sun

prevents heat build-up in the attic and, indirectly, in the downstairs living spaces. Proper attic ventilation is also necessary to prevent heat build-up.

Heat gain can also be controlled by eliminating or shading any large areas of pavement around the house. Otherwise they concentrate heat, as in thermal mass, or even reflect it directly into windows.

Cooling strategies should include natural ventilation. Windows and vents can channel natural breezes through the house. Even where there are no breezes, convective currents can be generated by placing vents in a high position, such as in a cupola, belvedere, or ridge skylight. The currents will not develop unless the height and size of the vent openings are carefully calculated and the outdoor temperature is cooler than the indoor temperature. High ceilings also help to keep a home cool by providing plenty of space for hot air to rise. A whole-house fan does the same job.

Other strategies are to relocate heat sources, such as water heater and clothes dryer, outside the living space and to install an exhaust fan in the kitchen. In hot, arid climates, concrete slab floors are helpful. Insulation and infiltration-control measures that are installed for winter heating will also help with summer cooling.

A final strategy for cooling is air conditioning. While central systems are most common in new construction, some homeowners prefer using one or two window units to provide spot cooling on very hot days, thus saving most of the cost of running a central system all summer. Air conditioning units are rated for energy efficiency. Select a unit with an energy efficiency rating of at least 100. Although efficient models may cost more initially, the long-range operating costs will make them worthwhile. Periodic maintenance, particularly the replacement of filters every two months, will help reduce operating costs.

Appliances

A new home offers an excellent opportunity for taking advantage of the energy-efficient appliances available today. They cost more, but the payback in long-range energy savings is appreciable. The initial cost can be rolled into the mortgage for the home. Presently, appliances and light fixtures account for about 10 to 25 percent of the average energy bill (more, if an air conditioner is included). The main energy users are the refrigerator, freezer, air conditioner, clothes washer, clothes dryer, dishwasher, and television. New products with high efficiency ratings can reduce energy use by as much as 50 percent for each appliance. "Energy Guide" labels will help you select the most efficient appliances.

Hot Water Systems

As the use of solar energy, insulation, and more efficient heating systems reduces energy consumption for new homes, the percentage of energy used for heating water increases proportionately. Water heating now accounts for about 20 percent of most energy bills, and will account for an even greater proportion as space heating and cooling systems become more efficient. In designing a hot water system for your home, you should select a high-efficiency unit. If your system is electric, consider installing a heat pump water heater, which works twice as efficiently as a standard resistance water heater. Also, make sure to include hot water conservation methods, such as low-flow showerheads and faucets.

Another way to provide most of your hot water is with solar water heating. The initial system cost is higher than that for conventional heaters, but should be more than compensated for by annual savings in energy use. Water heating is one of the most cost-effective of all home solar applications, and can be integrated into any home design with off-the-shelf components. As much as 75 to 80 percent of hot water needs can be met by a solar system. Higher percentages are possible, but not practical because of the enormous storage tank required. It is more feasible to install a conventional water heater in the system to boost temperatures and provide a back-up when needed.

Solar hot water systems operate on simple principles and have been used in many parts of the world for years. Most systems fit into two categories: active systems and batch systems. An active system heats water

in panels, called solar collectors, mounted on the roof and circulates it through a storage tank in the house or garage. The storage tank is larger than normal water heaters, usually 100 gallons. In most arrangements the system only preheats the water before it enters a conventional water heater. In others the circulating water can reach temperatures of between 120 and 160 degrees and can be used directly, although a back-up heater is still needed for extended periods of cloudy weather or high demand.

Collectors should face within 20 to 30 degrees of due south and have year-round exposure to the sun. The angle of tilt cannot always coincide with the angle of the sun, which changes throughout the year, but a good compromise for year-round heating is an angle equal to the local geographic latitude. If you do not plan to install a solar hot water system now, but think you might in the future, you may want to choose a home plan with at least one section of the roof pitched to the south to make it easy to install collectors.

The biggest problem with the operation of solar collectors is freezing. Even when nighttime temperatures are above 32 degrees, the water in a collector can radiate much of its heat to the clear dark sky and then freeze, bursting pipes inside. One solution is to use antifreeze in the collectors and use a device called a double-walled heat exchanger to transfer heat from the antifreeze to the domestic hot water. Propylene glycol antifreeze should be used instead of ethylene glycol, which will poison the domestic hot water if the heat exchanger leaks. Another way to prevent freezing is with automatic draindown valves that empty the collectors whenever the water temperature falls to a certain point or when the circulating pump is not on. This equipment is vulnerable to power outages because the automatic valve and sensors require constant voltage. There have been problems in the installation of draindown systems that have caused maintenance problems. In general, antifreeze systems have been more reliable.

The second major type of solar water heater is the batch heater, also called an integral collector system. The collector and storage tank are consolidated into one unit, so the sun heats the water storage tanks

directly. This simplifies the system. Some batch systems use one large tank inside the collector, while others use a row of 6- to 8-inch tubes to create a thinner collector with a lower profile. The storage tank or tubes are painted black to absorb solar heat more readily and are often treated with a special coating—a selective surface—that traps heat inside. The entire unit has an insulated glass cover to trap even more heat around the tank as well as to slow down heat loss at night. To keep

SOLAR HOT WATER

ACTIVE COLLECTOR SYSTEM

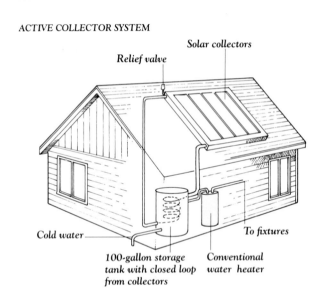

Relief valve

Solar collectors

Cold water

To fixtures

100-gallon storage tank with closed loop from collectors

Conventional water heater

BATCH SYSTEM

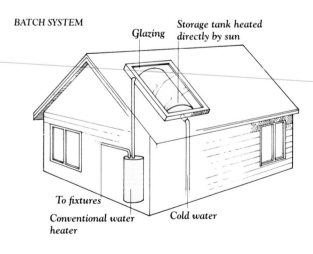

Glazing

Storage tank heated directly by sun

To fixtures

Conventional water heater

Cold water

the bulky profile of some of these units from looking awkward on a roof, most manufacturers offer stream-lined designs or units that can be recessed into the attic so that they resemble a conventional skylight.

Significant energy savings are also possible with conventional water heaters that use gas or electricity. High-efficiency models that get more heat out of the fuel are available. The cheaper cost of gas makes gas heaters less expensive to operate than electric heaters. Insulation for the tank and pipe, lower thermostat settings, and low-flow showerheads also increase efficiency. Your choice of other appliances also affects hot water usage. If the dishwasher has a booster heater to raise incoming water to 140 degrees or more, you can set back the water heater to between 100 and 120 degrees. A high-efficiency clothes washer with temperature and water-level controls will also save on hot water usage.

Special Features

lthough a sun-oriented home is really an inte-grated system of many ordinary building com-ponents all working together, there are two special features that by themselves can make almost any home more energy-efficient: sunspaces and "smart" technology.

Sunspaces

A sunspace, or greenhouse, is an appealing way to bring solar heat directly into the home. It creates an enchanting indoor-outdoor living space that capitalizes on breathtaking vistas or intimate garden scenes. It is a private, cozy world in the midst of the greater outdoors, where you can entertain friends or curl up with a book on a sunny winter day. This appeal, along with the wide availability of prefab kits, has made sunspaces very popular for new homes and older homes alike.

Sunspaces have a multitude of uses — lounging, dining, conversing, entertaining, exercising. They can be breakfast nooks bathed in early morning sunlight, or formal dining grottoes for sunset dinners. They can be

health spas for exercise and fitness, complete with a hot tub and exercise equipment. They can expand a living room or add an herb garden to a kitchen. They also make excellent air-lock entries.

Not all sunspaces are efficient solar heaters, and some are even net heat losers, depending on orienta-tion and design. But when used properly, a sunspace is an excellent way to tap solar energy. It allows a high concentration of south-facing glass when other areas of the same wall may not be suitable for solar gain. It benefits adjacent rooms. It concentrates potential prob-lems of heat loss, glare, and overheating in one space where they are easier to control. A sunspace can also help with summer cooling if it is designed carefully.

A sunspace on the north, east, or west side of the home will not contribute to solar heating. However, such a location may still be desirable for its architec-tural appeal. The potential heat loss will be minimized if the sunspace can be isolated from the living areas with weatherized doors and then used only during warm weather or occasional periods of direct sunshine. At other times, when sealed off from the rest of the house, the sunspace can act as a buffer against cold winter weather. It will even buffer against intense summer heat if vented properly.

To be an effective solar heater, a sunspace must be on a south wall of the house with the longest side fac-ing as close to due south as possible. It should have full solar exposure during winter months for at least four hours of the day. It should also be adjacent to as many daytime living spaces as possible — such as kitchen, family room, living room, or dining room — so excess heat can flow into them. Glass should be limited to the south wall; in the winter, other windows tend to lose more heat than they gain and tend to gain too much heat in the summer. This is especially true of overhead windows because they are tilted too far away from the needed winter sun and directly face the blazing summer sun. However, if overhead views of leafy tree canopies and starlit skies cannot be sacrificed, the roof glazing can be limited to a few skylights set close to the outside edge of the sunspace. The heat loss can be minimized at night with insulating devices and the heat gain controlled with exterior shades.

The size of a sunspace helps to balance the heat gain and loss. A width of 8 to 12 feet seems to be the most efficient. Length can vary, although sometimes it is more practical to add another elsewhere than to have one excessively large sunspace.

Multiglazed windows or other insulated glazing systems are essential for effective energy performance. Otherwise, the sunspace will be too cold on winter nights. Although an extra layer of glass reduces solar gain by 18 percent, it contributes to a net heat gain by reducing nighttime heat loss by 50 percent or more. East and west windows should be minimized, if used at all. Excess summer heat gain can be controlled by the use of tinted glass. Some sunspace designs have tilted

SUNSPACES

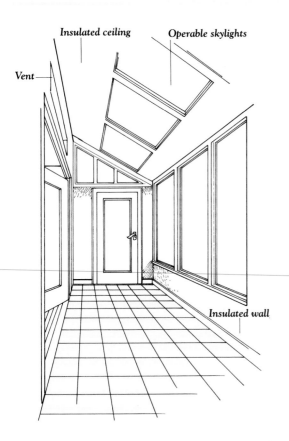

A sunspace admits warm sunshine during the day and can be closed off from the living space at night, acting as a buffer to reduce heat loss.

windows, others vertical. Tilted windows are intended to reach toward the sun, but vertical windows actually let in more sunlight when needed in winter because of the sun's low angle and the sunlight reflected off the ground. Tilted windows are also more difficult to insulate and shade, and more likely to leak. They should be used only when the angle is a desired architectural feature.

Heat from the sunspace can be distributed to other rooms by vents and doorways between the two spaces. A system of fans and ducts can be used, but is not generally worth the expense. When doors, tall windows, or vents are opened, a convective loop will force hot air near the sunspace ceiling through the upper vents into the living space. Cooler air from the living space will complete the loop by flowing along the floor into the sunspace through low vents. At night, the vents, windows, and doors should be closed so that the cooler temperatures in the sunspace do not draw warm air out of the house along the same path.

Heavy insulation and some thermal mass can prevent the sunspace from cooling rapidly on winter nights and cloudy days. However, too much mass keeps the sunspace from heating up quickly when the sun does come out because most of the solar energy goes into warming the mass instead of the space. For most climates, a concrete slab floor, paved with tile or brick, provides enough mass to modify the temperature swings. In cold climates, a well-insulated wood-framed floor may be better if there is not enough winter sunlight to heat the mass during the day. In some areas of the Southwest, where winter brings cold temperatures with sunny skies, the more mass the better. No matter what the climate, a sunspace should be well insulated and weatherized. The roof and walls, where there is no glazing, should be insulated to at least the levels required in the rest of the house, and insulation should be placed under the slab and around the outside of the foundation. Movable insulation for the windows or low-E glass may also be used, especially if the glass area exceeds 15 percent of the floor area of the sunspace and adjacent rooms.

If a hot tub or spa will be part of your sunspace, careful planning is necessary. When filled with water, a

Image labels: Insulated ceiling, Operable skylights, Vent, Insulated wall

spa adds thermal mass, which can absorb some of the solar energy needed for heating. It can also create problems with humidity if it isn't covered all the time. Large numbers of plants have the same effect (and need to be protected from low temperatures when the sunspace is isolated from the house at night).

Depending on how the sunspace is used, a back-up heating system may be necessary for extremely cold nights and prolonged periods of cloudy weather. The most common type is an electric baseboard heater, which is easy to install and can be maintained on independent controls. However, if the sunspace is to be used as much as a room in the heated area of the house, it should have a more efficient and less expensive form of heating.

Overheating in the summer can be controlled with shading. Deciduous trees and adjustable shades, either inside or outside, are the most effective. Skylight windows should be shaded on the outside to prevent heat build-up just beneath the glass. There should also be vents near the roof of the sunspace to send unwanted warm air to the outside, ideally with thermostatically controlled fans.

Many styles of sunspaces are available, either custom-built or assembled from prefab kits. Some have wood structures, others aluminum. Wood blends well with traditional architecture, but needs to be maintained to prevent weathering, splitting, and warping. Aluminum is more stable and comes in a small variety of colors, but may not blend with every home style and may aggravate the heat loss if it is not manufactured with a thermal break. Some hybrid systems combine the best features of both.

Kits, although expensive, are reliable and proven. They use glazing and sealing systems that are tested and refined, with warranties to back them up. They also offer accessories that are compatible with their designs, such as insulating and shading devices, doors, and fans.

"Smart" Homes

Electronic timers, remote sensors, relays for switches and valves, communication with outside networks, and other futuristic marvels can be used to automate many of the mundane and vital tasks in the daily operation of a home. Most people are aware of home security systems that automatically make phone calls, lights that turn on and off by themselves, and sprinkler systems that know when to water the lawn. These are just some examples of tasks that can be given over to "smart" machines.

Similar possibilities exist for streamlining energy control systems to make them more efficient than ever. For instance, shading devices operated by computers can adjust to changes in the sun's position, and heaters and air conditioners can be turned on and off in response to expected demand or available sunlight. Appliances can be programmed to operate at off-peak times, such as the middle of the night, when energy rates are cheapest, lights to turn on and off as people enter and leave rooms, and windows to open and close to regulate ventilation.

The newest innovation is to integrate all these operations (including devices not yet invented or dreamed of) into one complete system that can be operated from a central control in the home. Tasks are by no means restricted to energy conservation. A centralized system — or "smart" home — would also enable you to shop for groceries, order movies to play on the VCR, and have several newspapers delivered — all electronically.

The inventions of tomorrow should not dictate how a home is built today, but there are some simple ways you can anticipate future needs. One is to run extra wiring for telephone lines, computer links, speaker systems, and low-voltage switch relays. In the very near future, all these wires, along with standard electrical wiring, will probably be consolidated into one cable. The same cable will link all outlets in the house, so that one or several of the diverse appliances and fixtures — telephone, stereo receiver, toaster, security sensor — can be plugged into one of the jacks at any outlet. The functions will all be separated and sorted at a central terminal, allowing the integration of systems within the home and communication with networks outside. As you draw closer to starting your own home, consult with your contractor about integrating "smart" systems.

The Plans

THIS CHAPTER FEATURES HOMES THAT ARE DESIGNED FOR LIVING WITH THE sun. When these homes are oriented properly, their room arrangements and window placements offer an ideal combination of sun and shade. Each plan shows the best orientation for energy efficiency and pleasant living. A description of the sun's path through the house accompanies each plan, showing how the sun will affect various rooms during different seasons from morning through late afternoon.

The plans are grouped into three categories — Letting in the Sun, Enjoying the Sun, and Controlling the Sun. Each section presents a wide variety of home plans, including traditional Colonials and Cape Cod designs, ranch-style homes, and dramatic contemporary designs. Some are suitable for level building sites, others are designed for sloping sites.

Keep in mind that you can modify the plans shown here to suit your site or family needs. For example, you might change the orientation to put the morning sunlight in a different room or to take advantage of a magnificent view. In other cases, modifying the plan itself may get you the perfect design. The easiest modification is to reverse the plan. This means flipping the plan over so that, as you face the entry, the left and right sides are reversed. Holding the plan to a mirror will quickly show you what any plan in this book would look like in reverse. Plans can be ordered printed in reverse, but in some cases the writing will also be reversed, so an original set is also necessary for easy translating. Changing window sizes or moving the garage to the opposite side of the home are other modifications that generally do not require complex structural changes.

As you look through the plans, it will be easier to evaluate them and choose the most suitable home if you have clear criteria in mind. Some points to consider are the needs of your site and the overall size and exterior style you would like. When you have narrowed your choices to a handful of designs, you can evaluate the plans on their own merits, using a systematic checklist or other means to compare them.

Site Conditions

It is important to consider the main features of your building site when choosing a plan. They will determine which direction your home should face, where the driveway and main access should be located, and which direction the main window areas should face for the best solar exposure. The following checklist includes some of the site conditions that you should consider.

- On which side of the site is the street or road?
- Will the front of the home face the street?
- Should the entrance be on the same side as the garage?
- Which part of the site faces south?
- Is the north-south axis aligned within 30 degrees of the property line? If not, does the home have to be parallel with the property lines, or can it be rotated for ideal solar orientation?
- If the south side of the home faces one of the property lines, is there enough room on that side for a sunny yard?
- Are there any trees, buildings, hills, or other obstructions that would block the winter sun between 10 a.m. and 2 p.m.?
- Are there any large shade trees? Can the home be located so that the trees would be on the southwest, west, or northwest side of the house?
- Is the site level? If not, which direction is downhill?
- Will you want a basement?
- Where are the most pleasing views?
- Which part of the site is most suitable for a yard?

Daily Living Requirements

After you have selected a few plans that will work on your site, imagine what it would be like to live inside each home. Consider how the floor plan, the layout of rooms, the traffic corridors, the position of walls and doorways, the size of various spaces, and indoor-outdoor traffic flow will affect various activities. The inventory of your family's lifestyle suggested on page 33 and the guidelines below will help you get started.

- Are the shapes and sizes of rooms suitable for the furnishings you have or plan to get?
- Will noise — either from inside or outside the house — affect any of the quiet spaces?
- Will bedrooms provide enough privacy for the children as they grow older?
- Where will you put books and other collections?
- Where can family members go for privacy and quiet?
- Is there a place where everyone can congregate comfortably?
- Can children get from their rooms to the kitchen without going through the living room?
- Is there an office space?
- Does the garage have — or need — extra storage?
- Where will you watch television?
- Where will you entertain guests?
- What if you have a large party?
- What if guests stay overnight?
- Can visitors find a bathroom easily?
- What will the home be like after the children grow up and leave?
- Does anyone have special needs, such as wheelchair access?
- Can an adult cook and supervise children at the same time?
- Is the laundry convenient but out of the way?
- What if someone wants a late-night snack?
- Is the kitchen convenient to the decks and terraces?

- Is the front door convenient to the kitchen or other popular spaces?
- Where can family members enter when the weather is bad?
- Where can children play when the weather is bad?
- Are there appropriate places to display art?
- Is the fireplace located where you will use it?

Potential for Greater Energy Savings

When you have narrowed down your choices to several plans that you like, you may want to consider any additions or modifications that would make them more energy-efficient. At this point, it would be worthwhile to consult a solar designer or energy specialist about any such improvements. The list below suggests some additions or changes you might consider:

- Changing window sizes. For example, you might enlarge south-facing windows and reduce windows on the north side to minimize heat loss and on the west side to minimize summer heat gain.
- Enlarging or adding overhangs for summer shading.
- Adding solar panels on a south-facing roof slope for water or space heating.
- Adding or reducing a sunspace.

Trust Your First Instincts

Sometimes a plan will attract you instantly, and although you should consider the plan in much greater detail and not choose merely on impulse, do not discount the validity of your first reaction. The suitability of a home depends on your memories and dreams along with more practical considerations. Trust your intuition.

Letting in the Sun

he plans in this section demonstrate how you can let sunshine directly into a home to heat and light the interior spaces. You have a choice among many architectural styles and many exciting and creative designs, but they all share a common goal: getting direct sunlight to the maximum number of rooms or the largest possible floor area during winter months.

SUN-GATHERING HOUSE TYPES. The first group of plans, Sun-Gathering House Types, shows how conventional architectural styles can use south-facing walls, windows, and rooms to gain the most from the sun. Some of the designs take advantage of south-facing slopes to provide an additional floor level with full southern exposure. Others show how one- and two-story homes on level sites can open up to a southern exposure to maximize indoor sunlight.

SUN-ORIENTED ROOM LAYOUTS. The second group of plans, Sun-Oriented Room Layouts, shows how the layout of a home can be extended to multiply southern exposures. Various wings and shapes show exciting possibilities for gathering sunshine. Some of the plans include angles that limit the sunshine in the rooms to particular times of the day or year.

DRAMATIC WINDOW PLANNING. The third group of plans, Dramatic Window Planning, shows how imaginative window designs, thoughtful window placement, and bold roof openings can take full advantage of winter sun. In these homes, soaring windows, broad expanses of glass, and unusual skylights do not merely admit the sun — they welcome it with flair.

All the homes shown here will receive valuable heat and light from the sun, reducing dependence on conventional heating systems. Windows on the east, west, and north sides are minimized to reduce heat loss during cold months and heat gain during summer months. You will also notice how features such as the shape of the home and the location of the garage, closets, and other structural elements help control heat.

As you study the plans, note which rooms receive sunlight at various times of the day. Imagine your own family living in the home, and try to visualize how the floor layout and sun patterns would work for your daily activities. Where do family members spend time during the day? Which rooms will benefit the most from direct sunlight. Which should be protected from excess heat and glare? The caption for each plan will be useful for you in thinking about these questions.

Sun-Gathering House Types

This spacious contemporary opens up to the back for maximum southern exposure. An interesting array of shapes and angles on the back adds visual appeal and creates a play of light and shadow throughout the day. In addition to the main public spaces, three of the bedrooms receive direct sunlight. The breakfast room has a window on the east wall for morning sun, and a deck off the south-facing glass doors adds to the area's morning appeal. The same deck area is shaded from the late afternoon sun by the dining room. The decks and balconies also provide summer shading of many of the south windows. Note the centrally located kitchen and the whirlpool bath, which receives morning sunshine.

MAIN LEVEL
1096 SQ. FT.

LOWER LEVEL
1104 SQ. FT.

UPPER LEVEL
1115 SQ. FT.

DESIGN D2937
3,315 SQ. FT.
38,440 CU. FT.
4 BR, 3½ BA
FACES: N
SITE: SLOPES S

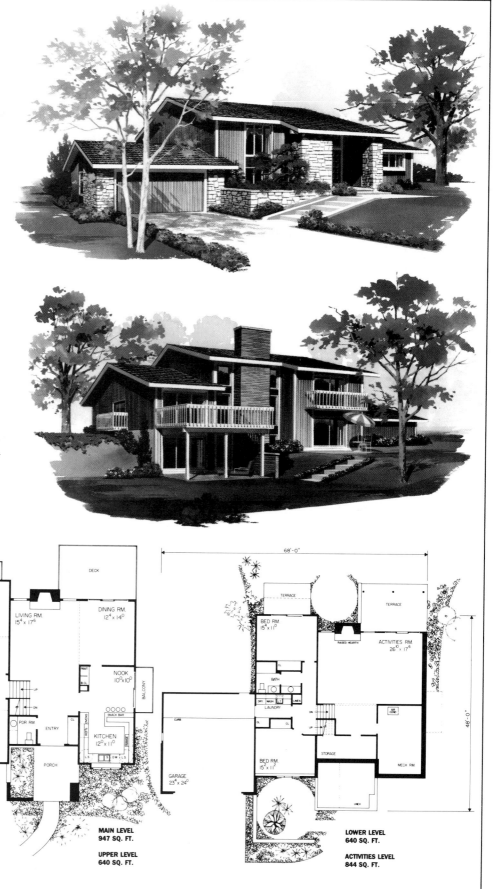

The spacious layout of this split-level contemporary is accentuated by the large window area facing south. The master bedroom, living room, dining room, and downstairs bedroom receive direct sunlight during the day, and the eating nook has a large window facing west. Balconies and roof overhangs shade the south windows. Observe the efficient kitchen layout, with a snack bar separating the working area from the informal eating area. The master bedroom suite includes a separate room for a retreat, nursery, or home office, with a north window for pleasant lighting. The downstairs areas offer abundant space for sleeping and daytime activities. Reducing the size of the upstairs deck would admit more sunlight into the activities room.

DESIGN D2763
3,071 SQ. FT.
34,090 CU. FT.
4 BR, 2½ BA
FACES: N
SITE: SLOPES SW

The elegant simplicity of this contemporary home lends itself to an ideal solar exposure. Every room has windows facing the back for direct solar gain during the winter. The north wall has few windows, and the west wall none, minimizing heat loss in winter and overheating in summer. Moreover, all the closets, bathrooms, and storage areas are aligned along the north wall, providing a buffer from north winter storms. The garage protects the west side of the house from summer overheating and winter storms from the west. The wall over the master bedroom closet has high gable windows to bring morning sun into the master suite. Note the soaring living room and foyer ceilings and the convenient access between kitchen and terrace.

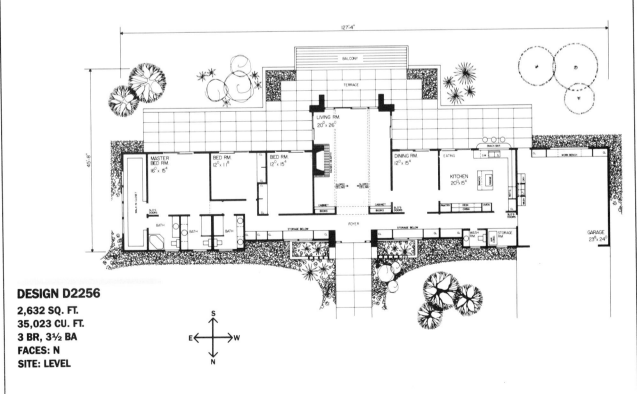

DESIGN D2256
2,632 SQ. FT.
35,023 CU. FT.
3 BR, 3½ BA
FACES: N
SITE: LEVEL

Three levels of south-facing windows on the back of this cheery home bring direct sunshine into every room. The gathering room has two levels of windows. There are few windows on the east and west sides, and the garage provides protection on the northwest corner of the home from winter storms. The angled deck dramatically connects the kitchen and gathering room and also serves to shade the downstairs rooms from the late afternoon sun. Note the two-story entrance foyer and the flexible arrangement of space in the lower level.

LOWER LEVEL
753 SQ. FT.

UPPER LEVEL
851 SQ. FT.

MAIN LEVEL
1044 SQ. FT.

DESIGN D2841

2,648 SQ. FT.
30,785 CU. FT.
3 BR, 3 BA
FACES: N
SITE: SLOPES S

Large windows grace the front and back walls of this elegant one-and-a-half-story home, making it possible to orient either wall toward the south for a sunny exposure. If the back faces south, the winter sun will warm the kitchen, family room, master bedroom, and two of the upstairs bedrooms, as well as the backyard terrace. The large front windows would bring indirect north light into the dining room, living room, study, and upper lounge during most of the year and direct sun during late afternoons for a few weeks in the summer. Facing the front toward the south would bring sunlight directly into these spaces most of the day and make full use of the dramatic two-story living room windows. The rooms and terrace at the back of the home would face north. With either orientation, only one window would face east or west, helping to control overheating during the summer and restricting winter heat loss.

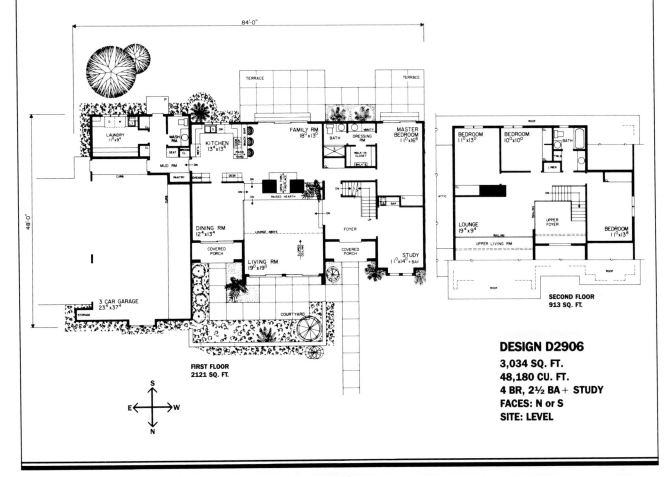

DESIGN D2906
3,034 SQ. FT.
48,180 CU. FT.
4 BR, 2½ BA + STUDY
FACES: N or S
SITE: LEVEL

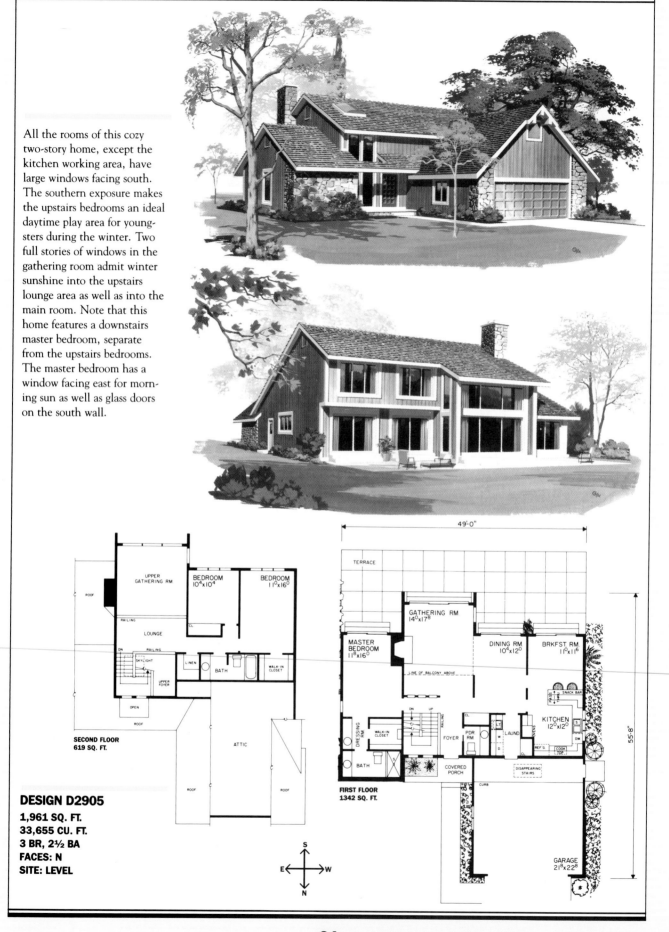

All the rooms of this cozy two-story home, except the kitchen working area, have large windows facing south. The southern exposure makes the upstairs bedrooms an ideal daytime play area for youngsters during the winter. Two full stories of windows in the gathering room admit winter sunshine into the upstairs lounge area as well as into the main room. Note that this home features a downstairs master bedroom, separate from the upstairs bedrooms. The master bedroom has a window facing east for morning sun as well as glass doors on the south wall.

DESIGN D2905
1,961 SQ. FT.
33,655 CU. FT.
3 BR, 2½ BA
FACES: N
SITE: LEVEL

SECOND FLOOR
619 SQ. FT.

FIRST FLOOR
1342 SQ. FT.

The hub of activity in this attractive contemporary is a central gathering room with two stories of windows facing south for maximum winter sunshine. This room is a step lower than surrounding rooms, so excess heat will travel easily into other areas of the house. Winter sunlight also floods the study, dining room, master bedroom, and one other upstairs bedroom throughout most of the day. The glass doors of the study admit sunshine until the early afternoon, when the protruding gathering room would block it. This makes the study a flexible work space, with morning sunshine for early starts and indirect light during the brighter part of the day. Adding a window to the east wall would bring in sunlight even earlier. Note how the upstairs lounge overlooks both the gathering room and the front entry.

FIRST FLOOR
1112 SQ. FT.

TERRACE

DECK

GATHERING RM.
14⁴ x 16¹⁰

STUDY
11⁸ x 11⁰

THRU FIREPLACE

DINING RM.
11⁰ x 10⁰

BOOKS

LAUNDRY

WASH RM.

KITCHEN
13⁰ x 10⁰

REF'G.

RANGE

FOYER

BRKFST. RM.
11⁰ x 7⁰ · BAY

COVERED PORCH

GARAGE
22⁰ x 21⁸ · STORAGE

STORAGE

ENT. COURT

54'-4"

49'-0"

S
E — W
N

MASTER BEDROOM
11⁸ x 13⁸

UPPER GATHERING ROOM

LOUNGE
10⁰ x 10⁴

BEDROOM
11⁰ x 10⁶

SECOND FLOOR
881 SQ. FT.

WALK-IN CLOSET

BATH

LINEN

BATH

ATTIC

UPPER FOYER

RAIL

BATH

CL

BEDROOM
11⁰ x 10⁶

DESIGN D2826
1,993 SQ. FT.
32,700 CU. FT.
3 BR, 2½ BA + STUDY
FACES: N
SITE: LEVEL

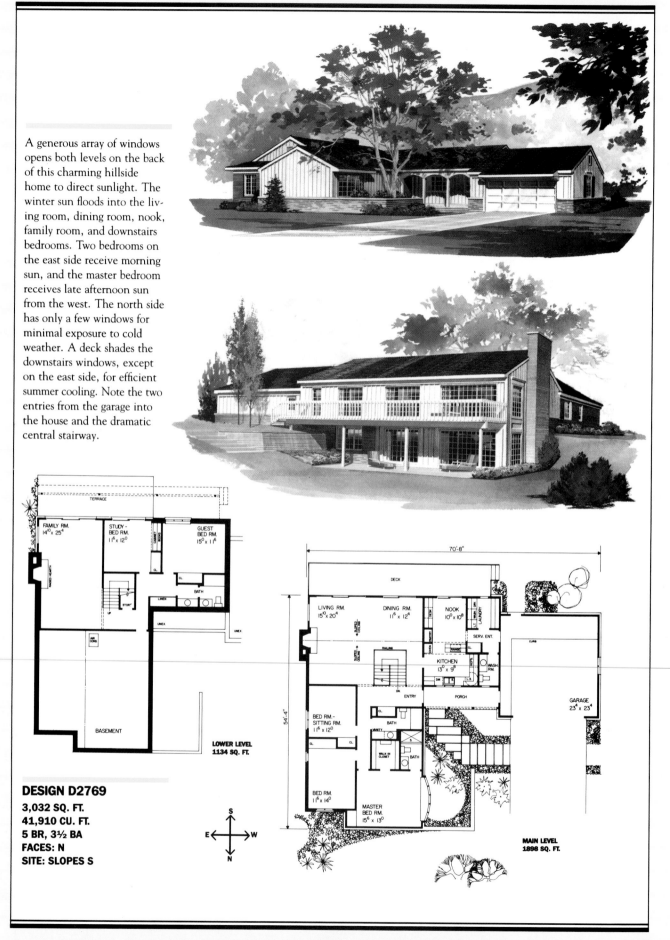

A generous array of windows opens both levels on the back of this charming hillside home to direct sunlight. The winter sun floods into the living room, dining room, nook, family room, and downstairs bedrooms. Two bedrooms on the east side receive morning sun, and the master bedroom receives late afternoon sun from the west. The north side has only a few windows for minimal exposure to cold weather. A deck shades the downstairs windows, except on the east side, for efficient summer cooling. Note the two entries from the garage into the house and the dramatic central stairway.

DESIGN D2769

3,032 SQ. FT.
41,910 CU. FT.
5 BR, 3½ BA
FACES: N
SITE: SLOPES S

LOWER LEVEL
1134 SQ. FT.

MAIN LEVEL
1898 SQ. FT.

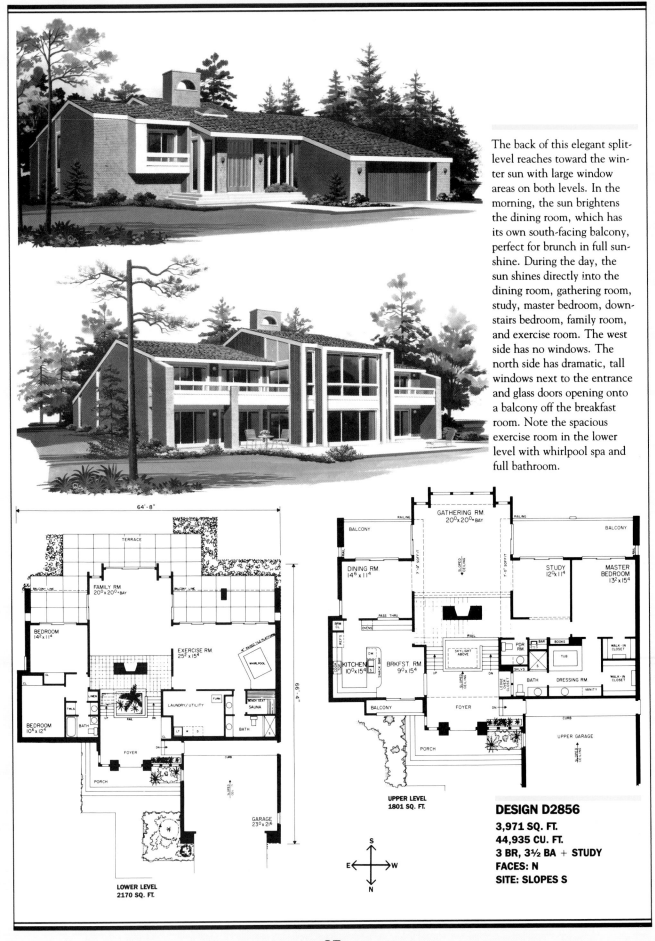

The back of this elegant split-level reaches toward the winter sun with large window areas on both levels. In the morning, the sun brightens the dining room, which has its own south-facing balcony, perfect for brunch in full sunshine. During the day, the sun shines directly into the dining room, gathering room, study, master bedroom, downstairs bedroom, family room, and exercise room. The west side has no windows. The north side has dramatic, tall windows next to the entrance and glass doors opening onto a balcony off the breakfast room. Note the spacious exercise room in the lower level with whirlpool spa and full bathroom.

DESIGN D2856
3,971 SQ. FT.
44,935 CU. FT.
3 BR, 3½ BA + STUDY
FACES: N
SITE: SLOPES S

The front of this hillside home is a one-story ranch, but the back opens up with two stories of south-facing glass. Throughout the day the sun shines into the dining room, living room, master bedroom, and two downstairs rooms. Decks, balconies, and the stepped-back profile of some of the rooms create a dramatic interplay of sunlight and shadow. Note the flexible spaces in the large basement and the through-fireplace between the living room and dining room. Reversing this plan would make it possible to put windows in the east wall of three bedrooms for morning sun.

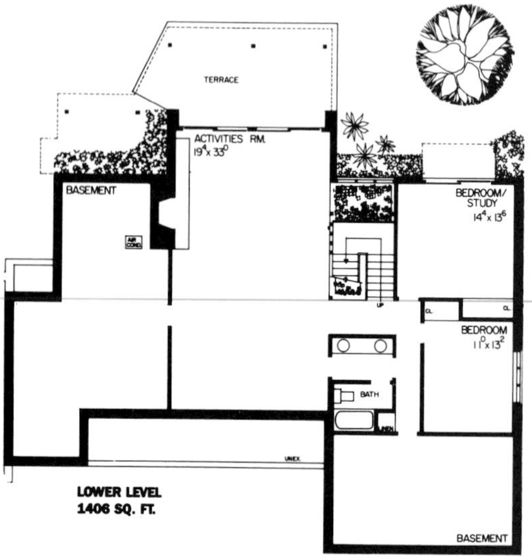

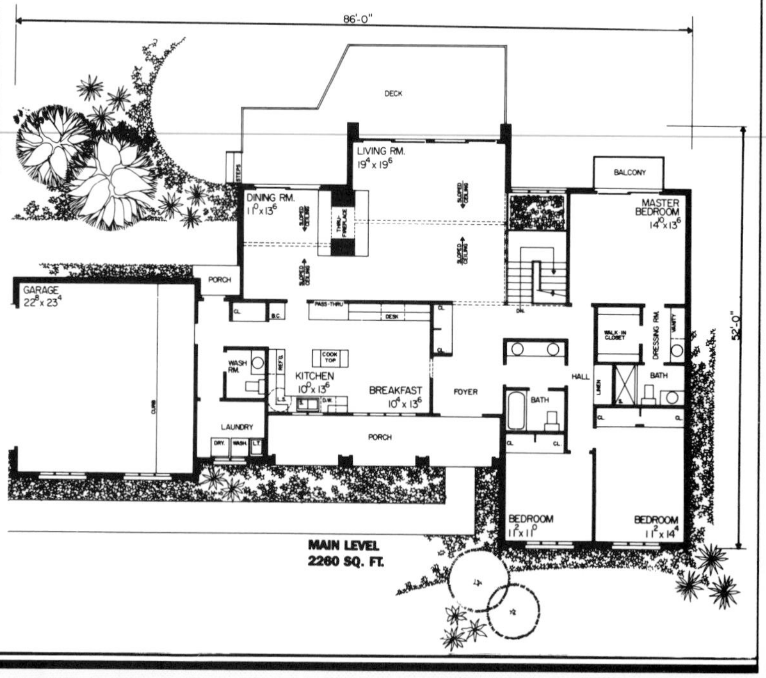

TERRACE

ACTIVITIES RM.
19⁴ x 33⁰

BASEMENT

BEDROOM/
STUDY
14' x 13⁶

AIR
COND.

BEDROOM
11⁹ x 13⁵

BATH

UNEX.

LOWER LEVEL
1406 SQ. FT.

BASEMENT

DESIGN D2549
3,666 SQ. FT.
51,857 CU. FT.
5 BR, 3½ BA
FACES: N
SITE: SLOPES SW

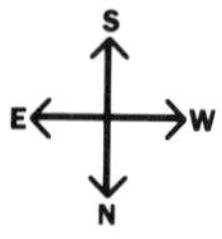

86'-0"

DECK

LIVING RM.
19⁴ x 19⁶

BALCONY

DINING RM.
11⁹ x 13⁵

THRU
FIREPLACE

MASTER
BEDROOM
14⁴ x 13⁶

GARAGE
22⁸ x 23⁴

PORCH

PASS THRU

DESK

WALK-IN
CLOSET

DRESSING RM.

VANITY

WASH
RM.

KITCHEN
10⁴ x 13⁶

COOK
TOP

BREAKFAST
10⁴ x 13⁶

FOYER

HALL

BATH

LAUNDRY

DRY WASH

PORCH

BATH

BEDROOM
11² x 11⁵

BEDROOM
11² x 14⁴

MAIN LEVEL
2260 SQ. FT.

S
E — W
N

This hillside home combines contemporary style with a bright, sunny interior. All rooms except the media room and game room have south-facing windows for direct winter sunshine. The garage, utility rooms, storage areas, bathrooms, and entry are aligned along the north wall. The east and west walls have no large windows, and the front of the home has a low profile for diverting north winds over the top of the roof. The north windows of the media room ensure diffuse light for TV viewing. Note the convenient kitchen layout between the family room and dining room, and the striking setting of the whirlpool spa in the master bathroom.

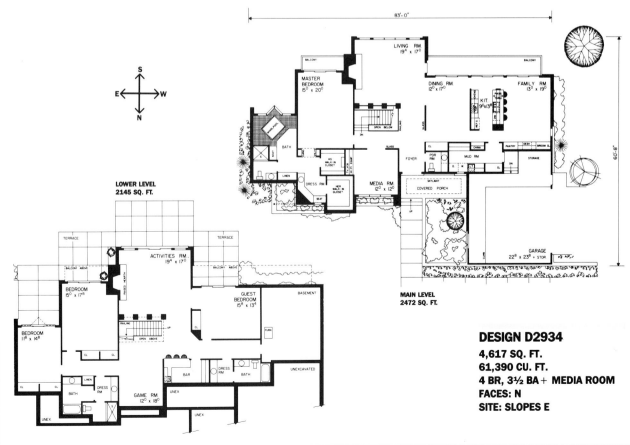

LOWER LEVEL
2145 SQ. FT.

MAIN LEVEL
2472 SQ. FT.

DESIGN D2934
4,617 SQ. FT.
61,390 CU. FT.
4 BR, 3½ BA + MEDIA ROOM
FACES: N
SITE: SLOPES E

Sun-Oriented Room Layouts

This elegant contemporary wraps around a central court-yard, with the main rooms at the back of the home opening up to a southern exposure. The breakfast room, dining room, and gathering room have east windows for morning sun. The dining room, gathering room, and study all face south for midday sun. The irregular profile of the back wall varies the solar exposure of these rooms, with the gathering room receiving continuous sun. Note the roof overhangs and support columns that help shade the south-facing windows from summer sun. The master bedroom receives late afternoon sun, and the central courtyard allows extra daylight into the interior portions of the home.

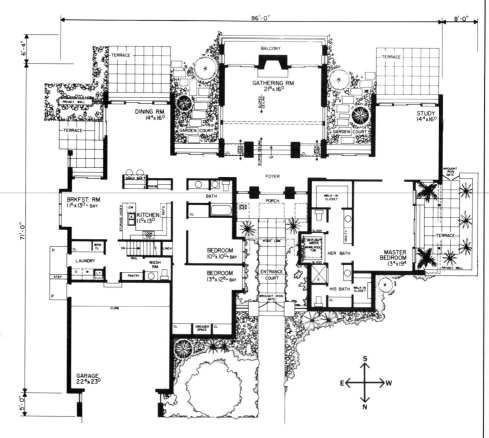

DESIGN D2857
2,982 SQ. FT.
60,930 CU. FT.
3 BR, 3½ BA + STUDY
FACES: N
SITE: LEVEL

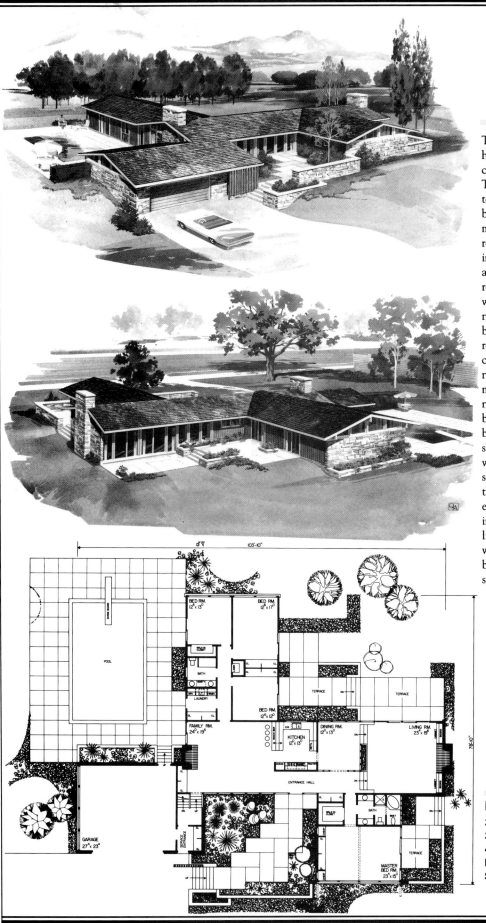

This striking ranch-style home has angled wings that create various solar exposures. The morning sun is restricted to the family room and main bedroom wing, but during the main part of the day the sun reaches into the kitchen, dining room, and living room. It also enters two of the bedrooms through upper gable windows. In the late afternoon it enters the master bedroom and two other bedrooms. The family room receives indirect light from the north. This home is best for mild climates where late afternoon sun is desired, perhaps because the morning sun is blocked by hills or overcast skies. The sunniest room would be the bedroom on the southwest corner. Orienting the home toward the northeast would bring sunshine into the main living areas earlier in the day, although it would no longer reach them by midafternoon. Note the sunken living room.

DESIGN D2251
3,112 SQ. FT.
36,453 CU. FT.
4 BR, 2 BA
FACES: N or NE
SITE: LEVEL

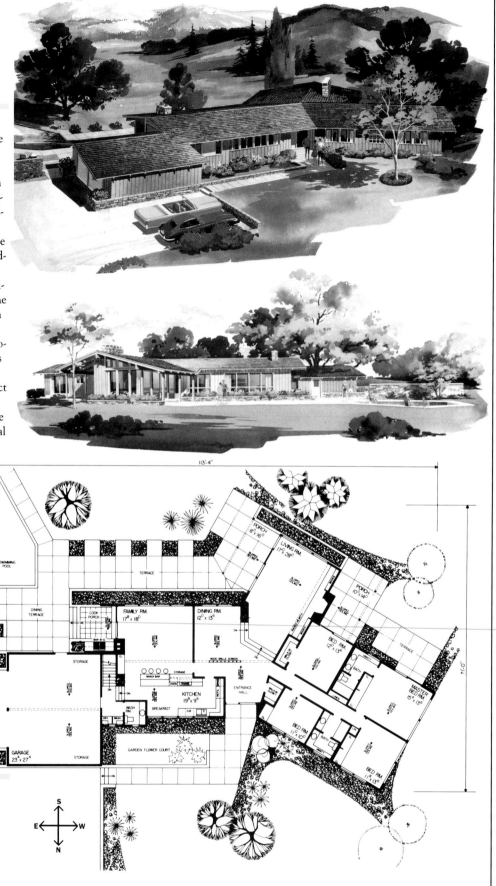

The sunken living room in this angular ranch-style home reaches out to capture sunlight during the winter. The family room and dining room also receive sunlight throughout winter days, and two bedrooms receive afternoon sun. Reversing the plan would face the windows of these two bedrooms, as well as the end of the living room, to the southeast for late morning sun. The family room and dining room would still receive midday sun, and the porch would protect the living room windows from sunshine later in the day. The garage would protect the west side of the home from hot afternoon sun. Note the sloped ceilings and special cooking porch for barbeques.

DESIGN D1223
2,568 SQ. FT.
34,762 CU. FT.
4 BR, 2½ BA
FACES: N
SITE: LEVEL

The angles of this ranch home create many possibilities for orienting it to the sun. With the front facing northwest, the kitchen and eating nook, dining room, and gathering room receive morning sun. The midday sun shines into the gathering room, study, and bedroom wing. If the back of the house is oriented due south, the kitchen area and gathering room receive sun for a longer period, but the bedrooms face the late afternoon sun in the summer. Reversing the plan brings morning sun into the bedroom wing and afternoon sun into the kitchen area.

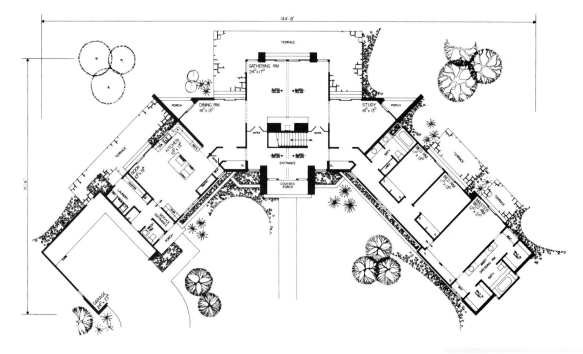

DESIGN D2534
3,262 SQ. FT.
58,640 CU. FT.
3 BR, 2½ BA + STUDY
FACES: NW
SITE: LEVEL

The rectangular shape of this charming traditional home orients rooms to the south and north and reduces exposure to the hot sun of the east and west. Rooms receiving daytime sun during the winter months are the master bedroom, kitchen, dining room, and large family room. A window could be added to the east wall of the master bedroom for morning sun. The rooms that face north — the living room, study, and two bedrooms — are not likely to require direct sunlight. The garage protects the west side from late afternoon sun during the summer and helps the utility area buffer the northwestern corner of the home from winter storms. Note the back-to-back fireplaces.

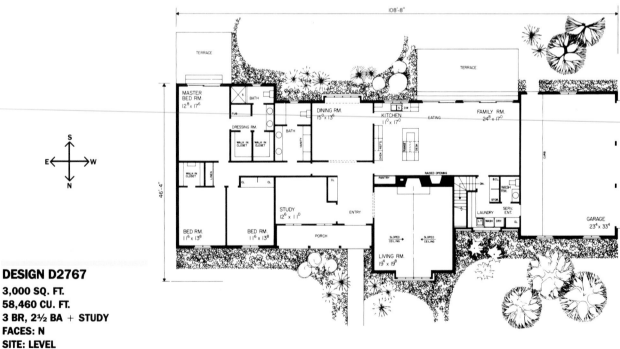

DESIGN D2767
3,000 SQ. FT.
58,460 CU. FT.
3 BR, 2½ BA + STUDY
FACES: N
SITE: LEVEL

This vacation home features generous window areas all around, with the main living spaces oriented so the living room faces southeast. The sun shines directly into the dining area in the morning, into the living area from late morning until midafternoon, and into the game area in the afternoon. The bedrooms on the west side would receive late afternoon sunshine during the summer. Reversing the plan would place the carport on the northwest corner of the home as a buffer against the late afternoon sun and bring the morning sun into two of the bedrooms.

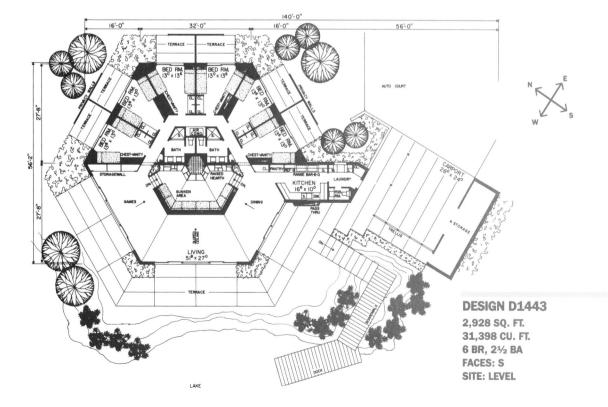

DESIGN D1443
2,928 SQ. FT.
31,398 CU. FT.
6 BR, 2½ BA
FACES: S
SITE: LEVEL

Two of the wings that wrap around the central pool and courtyard of this home can be oriented with the main windows facing south, bringing sunlight into the main living spaces during most of the day.

Two bedrooms and the family room have east windows for early morning sun. The study, master bedroom, dining room, and gathering room receive direct sunlight from midmorning until midafternoon. The

kitchen windows are shaded from the sun by the center wing until late morning, but receive sunlight until midafternoon. Note the windowed corridor along the center wing and the absence of west-

facing windows at the ends of the other wings. Almost all the rooms have windows on opposite walls, creating bright interior spaces that interact with the outdoors from almost any perspective.

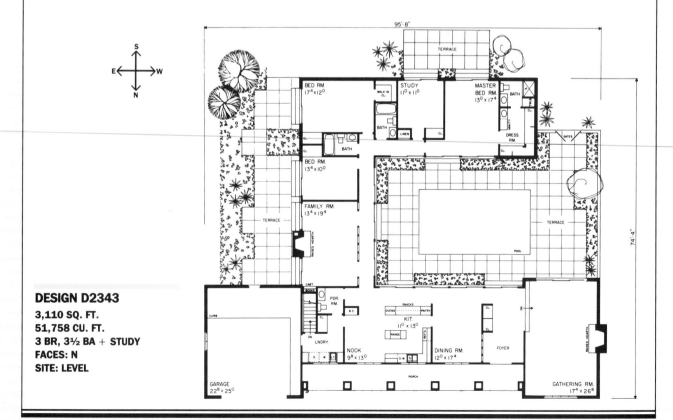

DESIGN D2343
3,110 SQ. FT.
51,758 CU. FT.
3 BR, 3½ BA + STUDY
FACES: N
SITE: LEVEL

Although this Western-style design works either way, reversing it east to west allows the best interaction with the sun. Three bedrooms, as well as the family room, would then receive morning sun. The kitchen, dining room, and living room would receive midday sun, and only the master bedroom would be exposed to late afternoon west sun. The garage on the north side would act as a buffer against winter storms. Note how the main living areas and master bedroom open out to courtyards and terraces and how beams and sloping ceilings enhance the main rooms.

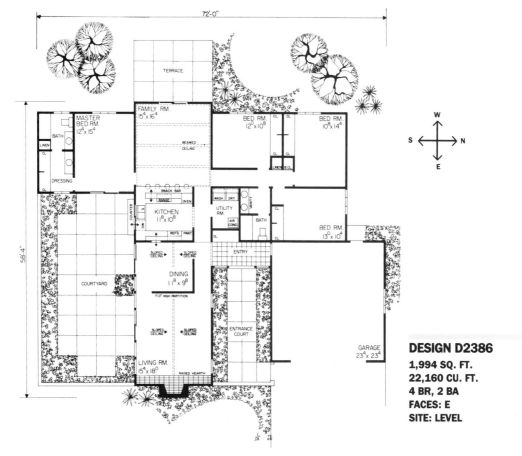

DESIGN D2386
1,994 SQ. FT.
22,160 CU. FT.
4 BR, 2 BA
FACES: E
SITE: LEVEL

The angle in this design allows several orientations. If the living room window faces south, two bedrooms receive morning sun, two bedrooms and the living room receive midday sun, and the kitchen and nook receive late afternoon sun. If the family room door faces south, two bedrooms still receive morning sun, the living room and family room receive sun throughout most of the day, and the kitchen is spared the hot afternoon sun of summer. The foyer, with built-in planter, routes traffic well. A pass-through counter separates the nook from the family room, which could also serve as a formal dining room. The north light of one bedroom makes it ideal for a studio or office. Note that the living room receives sunlight from two sides and has a raised-hearth fireplace.

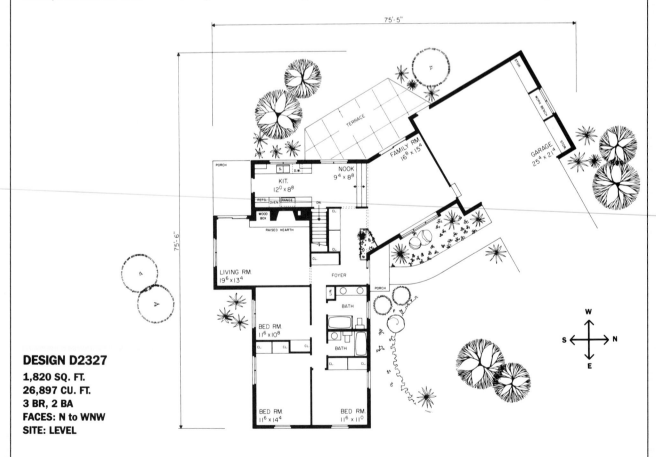

DESIGN D2327

1,820 SQ. FT.

26,897 CU. FT.

3 BR, 2 BA

FACES: N to WNW

SITE: LEVEL

The sweeping arc of this ranch-style home ensures maximum exposure to the sun. All the rooms except two bedrooms have windows or glass doors along the back wall, which should be oriented toward the south and southwest for optimum solar exposure. Morning sunlight enters the master bedroom through large windows on the southeast wall and also slants into the kitchen, dining room, and family room on the opposite side of the house through south-facing windows. These rooms receive full sun throughout the day. The living room receives winter sun in the afternoon, but in the summer a covered porch shades its windows. This porch could be enclosed with windows for a sunspace. The garage protects one wing of the home from northwest winter storms.

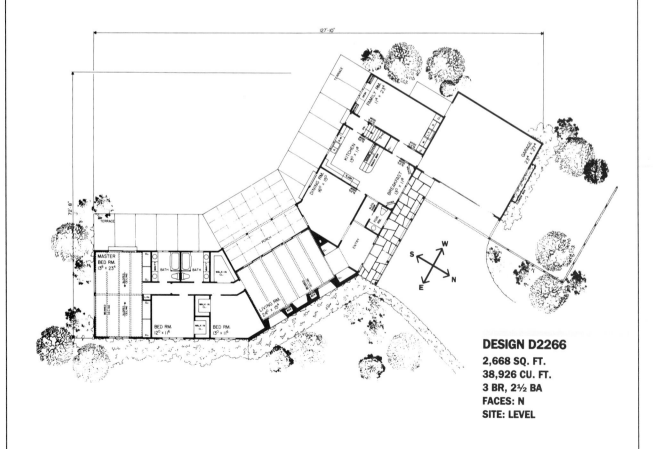

DESIGN D2266
2,668 SQ. FT.
38,926 CU. FT.
3 BR, 2½ BA
FACES: N
SITE: LEVEL

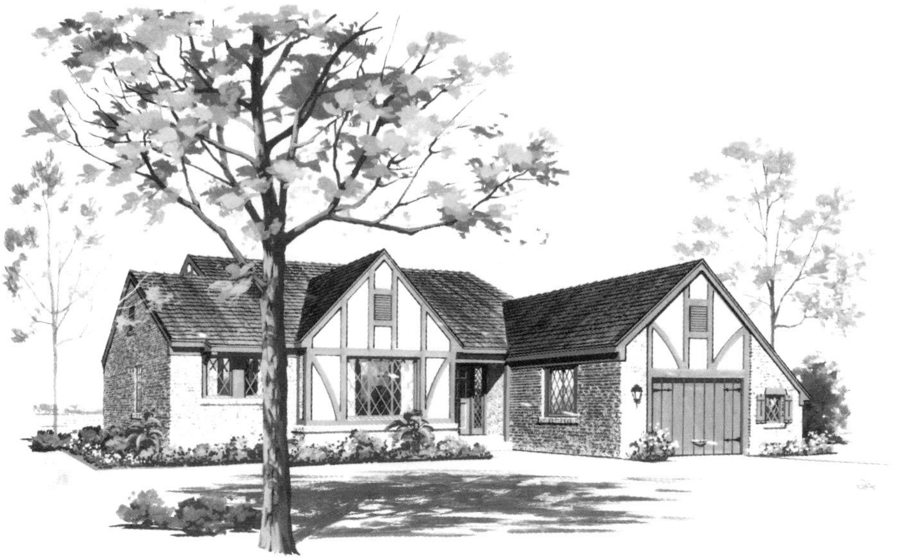

This Tudor-style home features a small sunspace off the study and a large area of south-facing windows across the back. During winter days the sun shines into the sunspace, master bedroom, gathering room, and dining room. Morning sun shines into the master bedroom and the sunspace. The kitchen and breakfast room have windows facing west for late afternoon sun. They would receive morning sun if the plan were reversed. The study, which provides a sunny place during the day, could be used as an extra bedroom. The masonry fireplace chimney in the sunspace provides extra thermal mass.

51'- 8"
TERRACE
TERRACE
SUN PORCH
SKYLITE ABOVE
SLOPED CEILING
GATHERING RM.
13⁴ x 16⁰
DINING RM
11⁴ x 10⁰
STUDY
10⁰ x 10⁰
SLOPED CEILING
BRKFST
11⁴ x 7⁴
TERRACE
MASTER BEDROOM
11⁴ x 14⁰
BAR
LIN
RAIL
DN
KITCHEN
11⁴ x 10⁰
OVEN
DESK
DW
BATH
REFG
RANGE
CL
FOYER
LAUNDRY
BATH
BEDROOM
11⁸ x 10⁸
COVERED PORCH
CURB
57'- 4"
GARAGE
13⁴ x 21⁸
STOR.

STUDY
M.B.R.
GATHERING RM
BRK
CABINET
BOOKS
AIR COND
BATH
KIT

OPTIONAL NON-BASEMENT

S
E
W
N

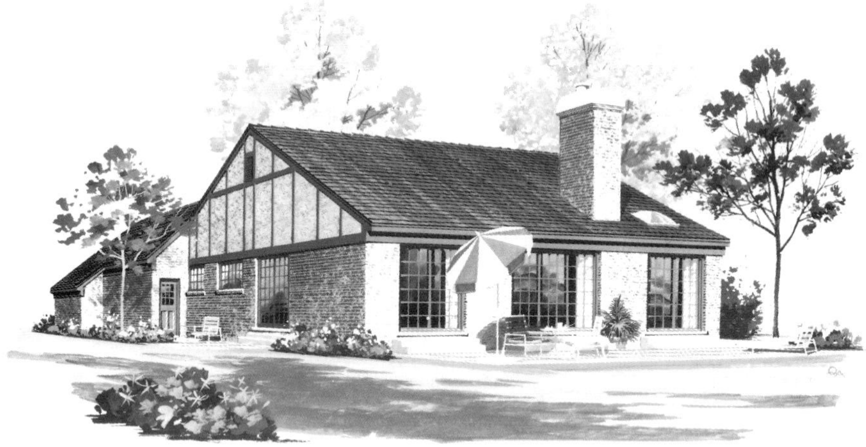

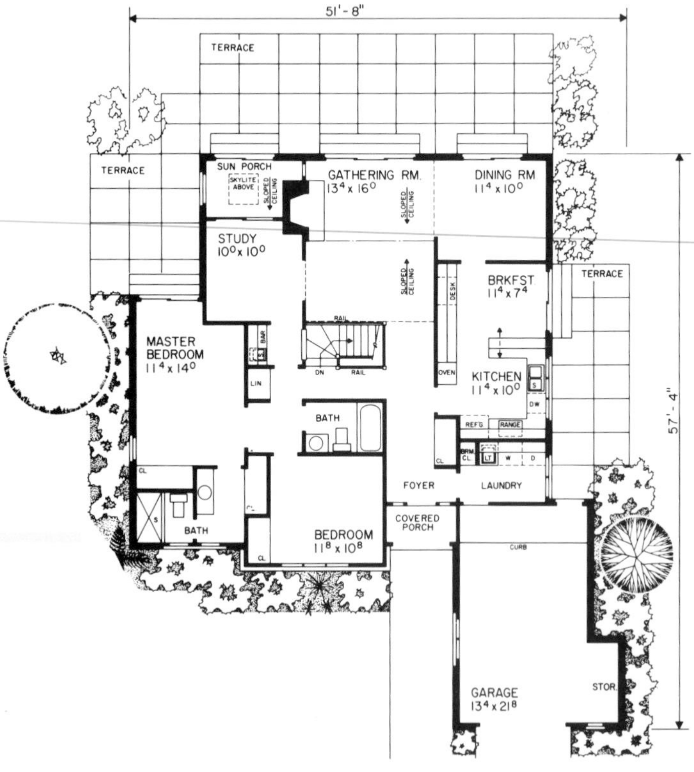

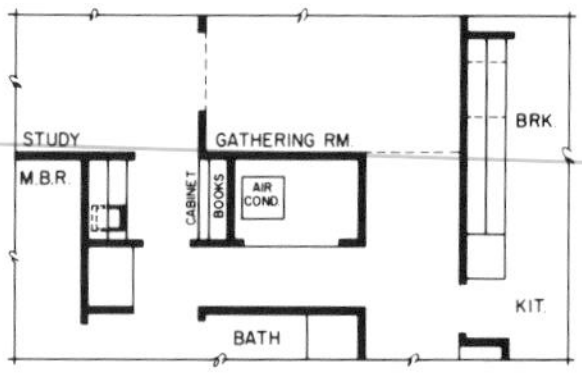

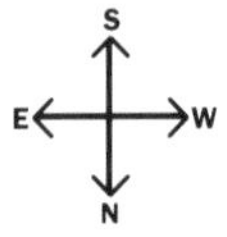

DESIGN D2825

1,584 SQ. FT.
34,560 CU. FT.
2 BR, 2 BA + STUDY
FACES: N
SITE: LEVEL

Dramatic Window Planning

Large window areas on two sides of this striking contemporary make it possible to orient the front to the north or the west. Facing north, it allows the master bedroom, dining room, breakfast room, and family room to receive most of the winter sunshine during the middle of the day. The family room, atrium, and two bedrooms would face west. If the front faced west, the master bedroom, dining room, breakfast room, and family room would receive morning sunlight. The day-time sunlight would flood the family room, atrium, and two bedrooms. The media room and living room would receive late afternoon sun in the summer.

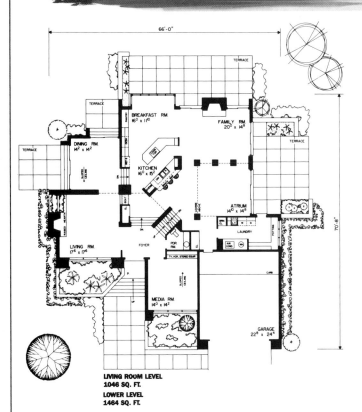

LIVING ROOM LEVEL
1046 SQ. FT.
LOWER LEVEL
1464 SQ. FT.

UPPER LEVEL
1570 SQ. FT.

DESIGN D2933
4,080 SQ. FT.
61,370 CU. FT.
3 BR, 2½ BA + MEDIA ROOM
FACES: N or W
SITE: SLOPES S or E

The back of this country Colonial opens to the sun with large windows and glass doors, including two bays for more visual excitement as well as more sunlight. The first-floor master bedroom suite is the featured room. It has glass doors facing east for morning sun, a large bay window facing south for sun throughout the day, and only one small window on the west side to minimize overheating. The large gathering room, breakfast room, kitchen, and two upstairs bedrooms also receive sunshine during the day, although the master bedroom suite blocks some of the windows from direct sun in the afternoon. The garage protects the dining room from late afternoon sun and buffers the house against northwest winter storms. Note the split-level terrace in the back, and the two fireplaces.

DESIGN D2695
3,239 SQ. FT.
49,765 CU. FT.
4 BR, 3½ BA
FACES: N
SITE: LEVEL

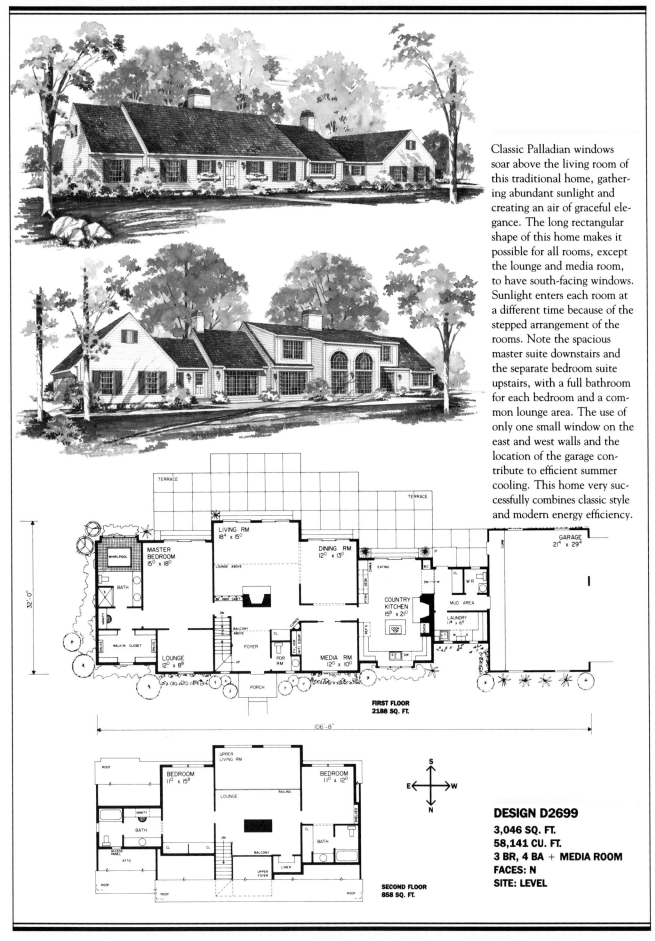

Classic Palladian windows soar above the living room of this traditional home, gathering abundant sunlight and creating an air of graceful elegance. The long rectangular shape of this home makes it possible for all rooms, except the lounge and media room, to have south-facing windows. Sunlight enters each room at a different time because of the stepped arrangement of the rooms. Note the spacious master suite downstairs and the separate bedroom suite upstairs, with a full bathroom for each bedroom and a common lounge area. The use of only one small window on the east and west walls and the location of the garage contribute to efficient summer cooling. This home very successfully combines classic style and modern energy efficiency.

DESIGN D2699
3,046 SQ. FT.
58,141 CU. FT.
3 BR, 4 BA + MEDIA ROOM
FACES: N
SITE: LEVEL

This contemporary, clustered around a small courtyard, has the friendly feeling of a village. Sloped ceilings, open spaces, and unexpected windows enhance the drama of natural sunlight as it darts in and out of various rooms throughout the day. Even the breakfast room on the west side can receive some morning sun from the atrium. The north-facing family room is lit from two sides, and all four bedrooms have east windows for morning sun. Note the open trellis over the inviting entry garden and the generous storage spaces throughout.

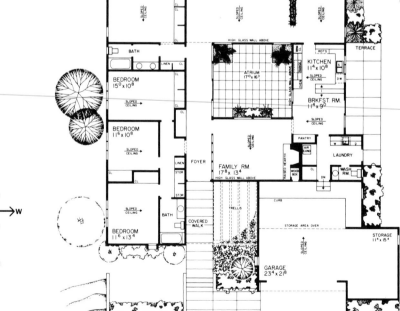

DESIGN D2135
2,495 SQ. FT.
28,928 CU. FT.
4 BR, 2½ BA
FACES: N
SITE: LEVEL

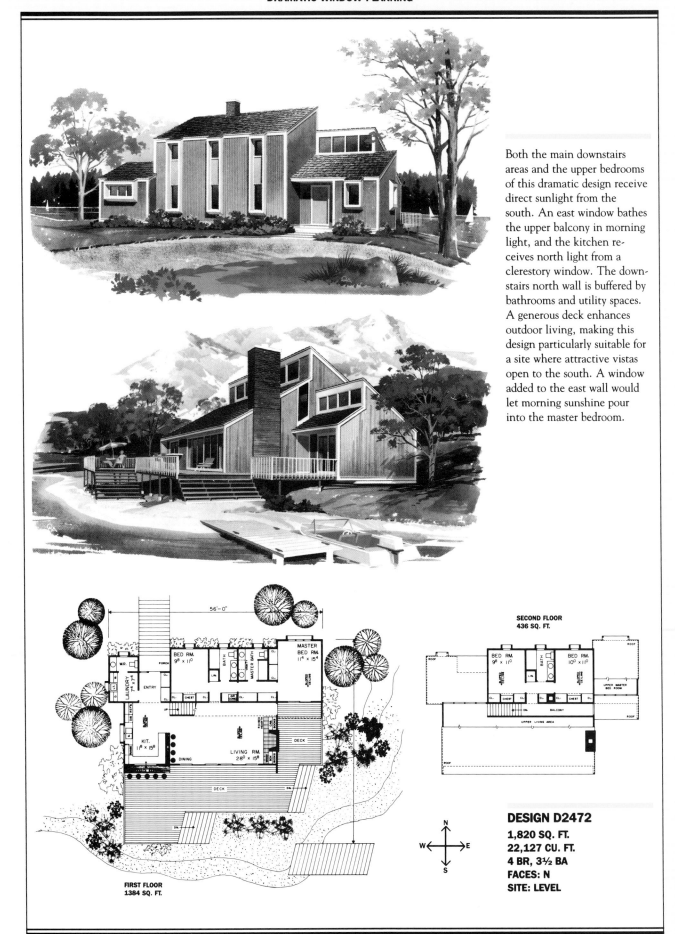

Both the main downstairs areas and the upper bedrooms of this dramatic design receive direct sunlight from the south. An east window bathes the upper balcony in morning light, and the kitchen receives north light from a clerestory window. The downstairs north wall is buffered by bathrooms and utility spaces. A generous deck enhances outdoor living, making this design particularly suitable for a site where attractive vistas open to the south. A window added to the east wall would let morning sunshine pour into the master bedroom.

SECOND FLOOR
436 SQ. FT.

FIRST FLOOR
1384 SQ. FT.

DESIGN D2472
1,820 SQ. FT.
22,127 CU. FT.
4 BR, 3½ BA
FACES: N
SITE: LEVEL

A striking three-story window well in the back of this contemporary home floods the gathering room and activities room with direct sunlight. The master bedroom lounge, dining room, study, and exercise room also have south-facing windows for direct solar exposure. The kitchen features a circular breakfast room with windows facing east and southeast for morning sun. Lack of windows on the west wall prevents late afternoon overheating. Note the private balconies for the study and master bedroom, and the stair landing at the master bedroom level that overlooks the main gathering room.

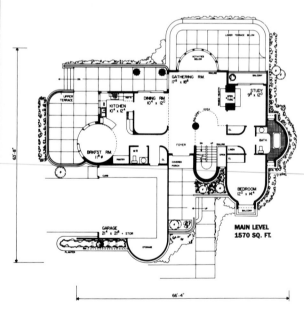

MAIN LEVEL
1570 SQ. FT.

LOWER LEVEL
1080 SQ. FT.

UPPER LEVEL
598 SQ. FT.

DESIGN D2926
3,248 SQ. FT.
42,114 CU. FT.
2 BR, 3½ BA + STUDY
FACES: N
SITE: LEVEL

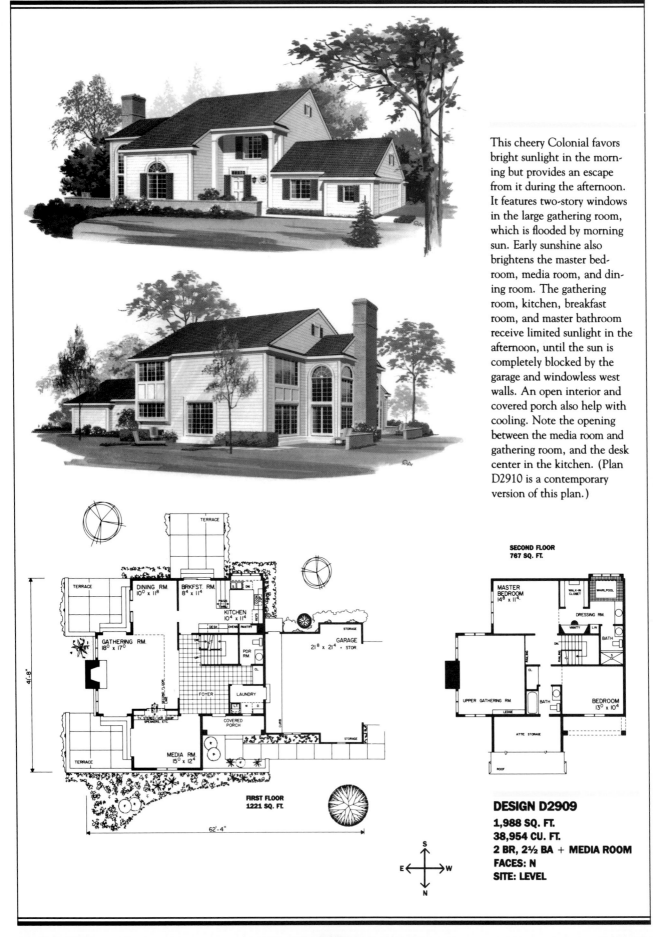

This cheery Colonial favors bright sunlight in the morning but provides an escape from it during the afternoon. It features two-story windows in the large gathering room, which is flooded by morning sun. Early sunshine also brightens the master bedroom, media room, and dining room. The gathering room, kitchen, breakfast room, and master bathroom receive limited sunlight in the afternoon, until the sun is completely blocked by the garage and windowless west walls. An open interior and covered porch also help with cooling. Note the opening between the media room and gathering room, and the desk center in the kitchen. (Plan D2910 is a contemporary version of this plan.)

SECOND FLOOR
767 SQ. FT.

FIRST FLOOR
1221 SQ. FT.

DESIGN D2909
1,988 SQ. FT.
38,954 CU. FT.
2 BR, 2½ BA + MEDIA ROOM
FACES: N
SITE: LEVEL

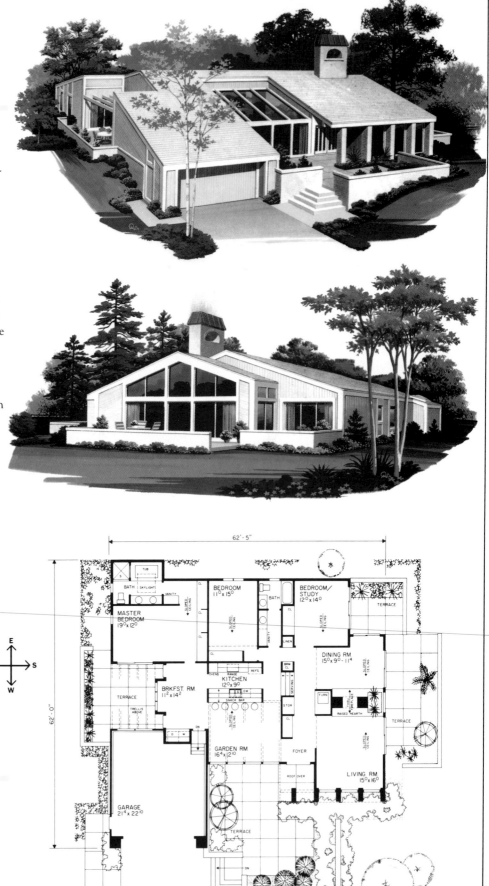

With the entry of this clean-lined contemporary facing west, the large glass gable over the living room and dining room windows increases the direct sunshine available to those rooms. The garden room would face west, bringing late afternoon sun to the adjacent kitchen, breakfast room, and living room. The plan could be reversed, if overheating might be a problem, so that the garden room faces east instead of west. The home would then have an east entry, with morning sun flooding the kitchen area; the living and dining rooms would still receive midday sun in winter. Another possible orientation is to face the entry to the south (without reversing the plan). Morning sunlight would flood the living and dining room areas, the garden room would receive midday sun, and the bedrooms would be aligned along the north wall for cool sleeping. Note the skylight over the master bath.

DESIGN D2858

2,231 SQ. FT.
28,150 CU. FT.
3 BR, 2 BA
FACES: S or W
SITE: LEVEL

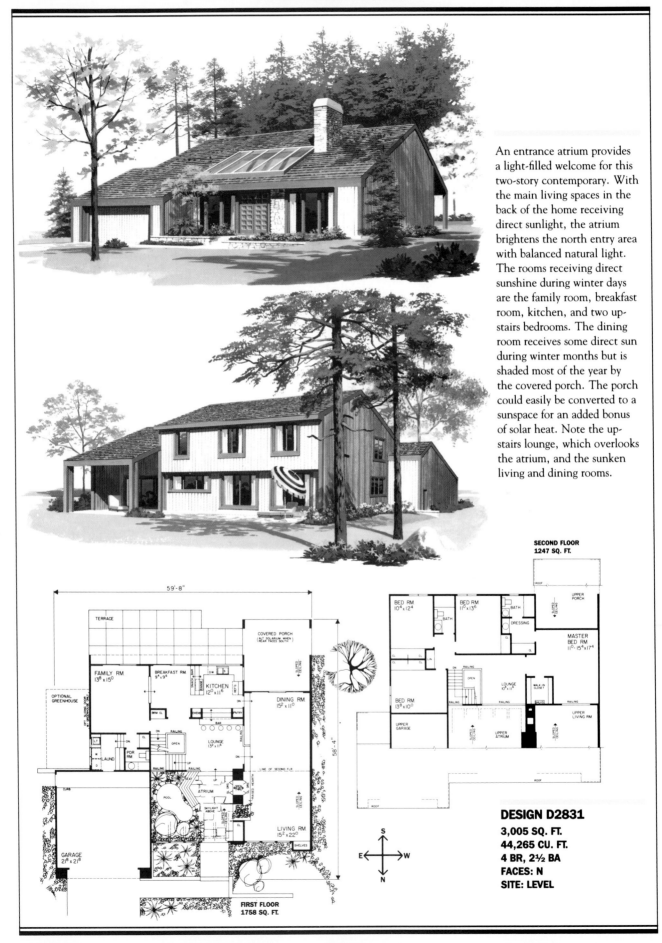

An entrance atrium provides a light-filled welcome for this two-story contemporary. With the main living spaces in the back of the home receiving direct sunlight, the atrium brightens the north entry area with balanced natural light. The rooms receiving direct sunshine during winter days are the family room, breakfast room, kitchen, and two upstairs bedrooms. The dining room receives some direct sun during winter months but is shaded most of the year by the covered porch. The porch could easily be converted to a sunspace for an added bonus of solar heat. Note the upstairs lounge, which overlooks the atrium, and the sunken living and dining rooms.

SECOND FLOOR
1247 SQ. FT.

DESIGN D2831
3,005 SQ. FT.
44,265 CU. FT.
4 BR, 2½ BA
FACES: N
SITE: LEVEL

FIRST FLOOR
1758 SQ. FT.

All the major rooms of this earth-sheltered home receive sunlight through windows facing south or east. The kitchen and dining room receive morning sun through east windows, as well as daylight from the atrium skylight. The gathering room and dining room are sunny all day. Protruding walls outside the three bedrooms block the sun except during the middle of the day. Earth berms on the west and north walls help to conserve heat in the winter and maintain cool temperatures in the summer. Note that bathrooms and utility spaces are concentrated along the north wall to provide a buffer and that both the east and south walls have overhangs to shade the windows.

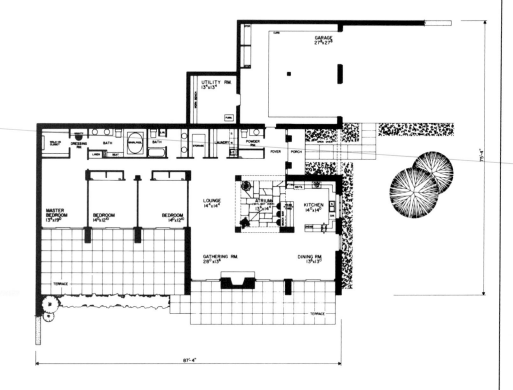

DESIGN D2863
2,955 SQ. FT.
30,387 CU. FT.
3 BR, 2½ BA
FACES: E
SITE: LEVEL

Whether your lot is on the sunny side of the street or the shady side, this charming traditional home is a solar winner either way. If it is oriented to the north, the main rooms in the back of the home and two upstairs bedrooms would receive direct sun throughout the day during the winter. The study, eating nook, and one bedroom would face north and receive diffuse light. Because there are no windows on the sides, it is possible to reverse the orientation so the front faces south. The front windows would gain enough direct solar exposure to offset the larger north-facing glass doors in the back of the house. This would create a sunny kitchen and nook area.

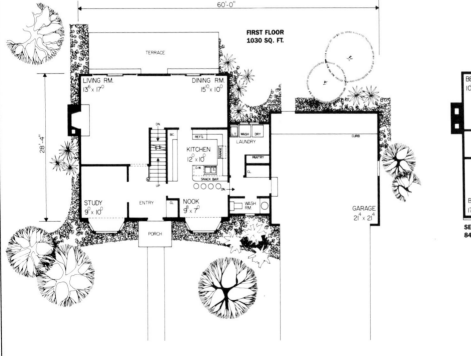

SECOND FLOOR
840 SQ. FT.

DESIGN D2558
1,870 SQ. FT.
27,120 CU. FT.
3 BR, 2½ BA + STUDY
FACES: N or S
SITE: LEVEL

A central covered atrium is the source of sunlight for most of the interior of this stunning contemporary home. South-facing glass doors in the living room admit direct sunshine during winter months, and the west-facing glass doors of the dining room open that room to afternoon sun. The atrium is at the same level as the bedroom wing, but the living room, dining room, and kitchen are a step higher. This construction makes possible the sunken conversation area in the living room. On a site where extensive window areas are not possible because of limited privacy or obstructed solar exposure, this home would be ideal.

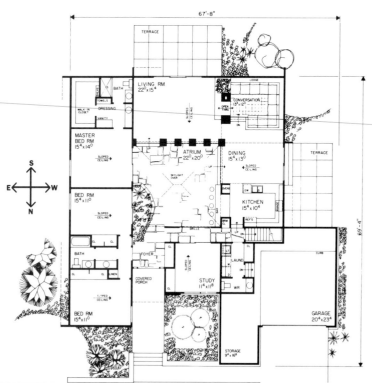

DESIGN D2832
2,803 SQ. FT.
52,235 CU. FT.
3 BR, 2½ BA + STUDY
FACES: N
SITE: LEVEL

This stately Colonial begins the day with sunlight streaming into the upstairs master bedroom, the large country kitchen and adjacent dining room, and two east windows of the great room. During the day it shines into the dining room, great room, and one bedroom. The tall window wall of the great room admits sunlight deep into the room, reaching the upstairs balcony. Two bedrooms have windows facing west for late afternoon sun. The spacious master suite has a curved balcony overlooking the entry foyer. Note the upstairs lounge, the convenient laundry in the upstairs bathroom, and the separate library.

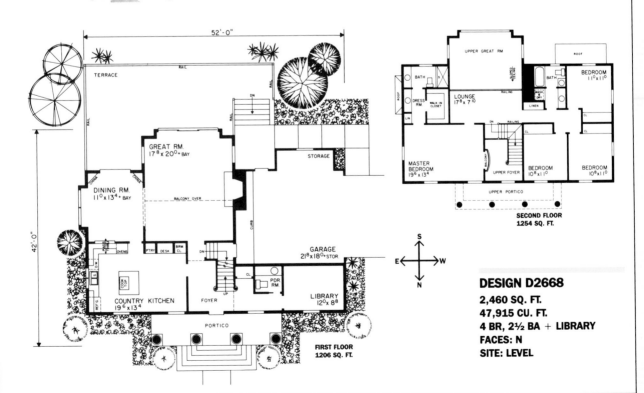

DESIGN D2668
2,460 SQ. FT.
47,915 CU. FT.
4 BR, 2½ BA + LIBRARY
FACES: N
SITE: LEVEL

With the side entry of this dramatic vacation home facing east, the soaring glass prow opens both levels to direct sunlight from the south. Glass doors on the east admit morning sun into the entry area and upstairs master bath. All the bedrooms have windows facing north. The roof shades most of the south windows for part of the summer, and during the winter the main living area is flooded with warm sunshine. Note the separate master suite upstairs, which boasts a private deck and an interior balcony overlooking the main living area.

DESIGN D2431
1,463 SQ. FT.
15,230 CU. FT.
3 BR, 2 BA
FACES: E
SITE: LEVEL

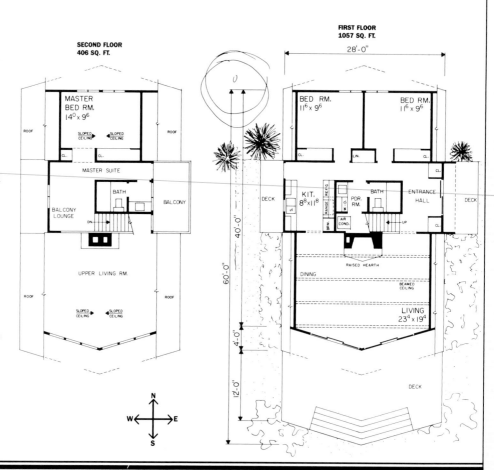

SECOND FLOOR
406 SQ. FT.

ROOF

MASTER
BED RM.
14⁰ x 9⁶

SLOPED CEILING   SLOPED CEILING

CL.   CL.

ROOF

MASTER SUITE

BALCONY LOUNGE

BATH

BALCONY

DN.

UPPER LIVING RM.

ROOF

ROOF

SLOPED CEILING   SLOPED CEILING

FIRST FLOOR
1057 SQ. FT.

28'-0"

BED RM.
11⁶ x 9⁶

BED RM.
11⁶ x 9⁶

CL.   LIN.   CL.

DECK

KIT.
8⁸ x 11⁸

PDR. RM.

BATH

ENTRANCE HALL

DECK

AIR COND.

RANGE   REFG.

W.   D.

CL.

UP

RAISED HEARTH

DINING

BEAMED CEILING

LIVING
23⁴ x 19⁴

DECK

40'-0"   60'-0"   4'-0"   12'-0"

N
W   E
S

Enjoying the Sun

lanning a home around the sun can go further than just using the sun for heat and light. It can extend to planning special places where you can rest and revel in the sun every season of the year. Sunspaces, decks, balconies, and terraces as extensions of living space help you celebrate the sun.

You might enjoy the benefits of an enclosed sunspace, an indoor-outdoor environment that offers the best of solar living with the convenience of indoor living. Examples are illustrated in the first two groups of plans.

SUNSPACES FOR COMFORTABLE LIVING. The first group of plans, Sunspaces for Comfortable Living, features sunspaces suitable for leisure and relaxation. These sunspaces may be located off a living room, bedroom, family room, or dining room, supplying a comfortable area for conversing, entertaining, reading, relaxing, or enjoying the outdoor view. They can be elegant and luxurious or warm and casual. These spaces enhance both the indoor livability and the outdoor appearance of your home.

SUNSPACES TO BRIGHTEN WORK AREAS. The second group of plans, Sunspaces to Brighten Work Areas, incorporates sunspaces in the more utilitarian areas of the home — the kitchen, eating, and service areas. These are areas where families often spend a great deal of time, so why not brighten them with sunshine?

SUNSPACES FOR OUTDOOR AREAS. If you enjoy the sun without the intervention of protective walls, you will be interested in the third group of plans, Sunspaces for Outdoor Areas. These homes feature decks, balconies, and terraces that are convenient to living areas within the home. Most of these outdoor spaces have full exposure to the sun, but some are designed to supply a shady spot outdoors. Many of these homes feature both shaded and sunny outdoor areas.

The plans in this section feature special spaces for enjoying the sun, but they do not neglect the use of the sun in other parts of the house. These plans feature room arrangements, window placement, and orientations that bring the sun into many rooms.

Sunspaces for Comfortable Living

The sheltered front of this elegant contemporary is snug and tight against winter storms, while the large windows of the back open up to warm sunshine during winter days. Early morning sunlight greets the working person in the study, and the breakfast room has a window seat facing west — great for watching sunsets after work. Note the wide roof overhang with a skylight outside the gathering room. It could be narrowed for more winter sunshine, or easily enclosed for an ideal sunspace. The lower level of the gathering room would help heat from the sunspace rise toward the other rooms on the main floor.

SECOND FLOOR 927 SQ. FT.

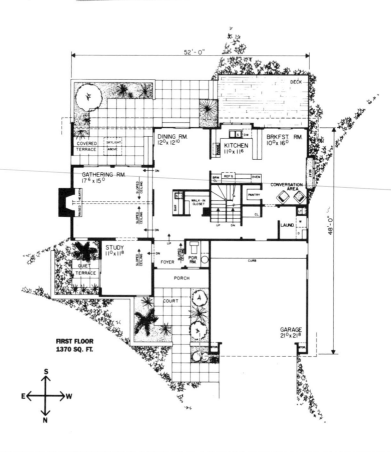

FIRST FLOOR 1370 SQ. FT.

DESIGN D2823
2,297 SQ. FT.
34,860 CU. FT.
3 BR, 2½ BA + STUDY
FACES: N
SITE: SLOPES E

The country feeling of this elegant Colonial suits the spacious, sunny interior. The upstairs bedrooms, master bedroom, sunspace, dining room, kitchen, and family room all have south windows for maximum winter sunshine. The sunspace is perfectly located for distributing heat into the adjacent rooms and can be closed off at night whenever necessary. One bedroom has windows facing north, which makes it ideal for a daytime study or work space. Note the placement of the garage for protection from northwest storms and the convenient location of the kitchen between dining room and family room.

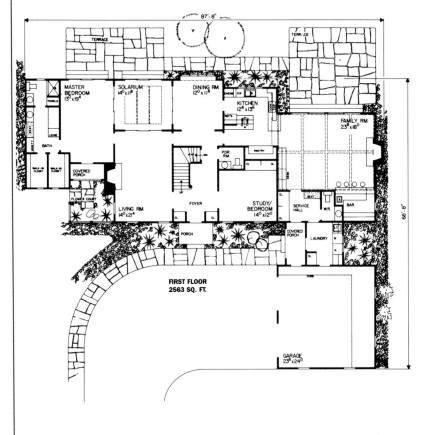

DESIGN D2615
3,115 SQ. FT.
59,513 CU. FT.
4 BR, 2½ BA
FACES: N
SITE: LEVEL

A sunspace tucked in the corner between the living and dining rooms could add bonus heat to the rest of this home. The living room and master bedroom also receive direct sunlight during winter days. One bedroom receives morning sun, but the master bedroom could also gain morning sun through a window placed in the east wall. Note how the garage faces west for flexible access and how it protects the northwest corner of the house. Other features of this handsome contemporary include a beamed terrace off the breakfast room, a kitchen greenhouse window, effective zoning of public and private spaces, and a front bedroom with large north windows, ideal for a studio or office.

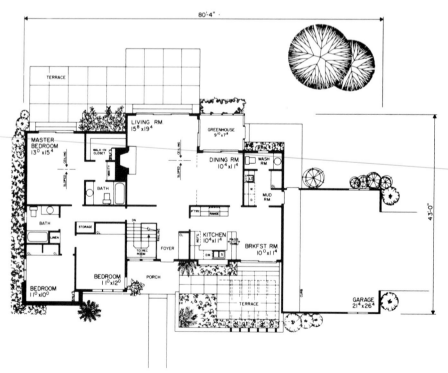

DESIGN D2871

1,905 SQ. FT.
44,590 CU. FT.
3 BR, 2½ BA
FACES: N
SITE: LEVEL

This attractive contemporary features a two-story sunspace in the back. Light and heat flow from the sunspace into upstairs bedrooms, the family room, and the main hallway. The bedrooms, master bathroom, and family room have south windows for direct sun during the winter. The family room also has west windows, and the kitchen has a small sunspace facing southwest. The dining room, living room, and study face north. The garage helps to protect the northwest corner of the home from winter winds. Note the sunken living room and study with private access to the master bedroom.

SUNSPACE 551 SQ. FT.

SECOND FLOOR 953 SQ. FT.

76'-8"

65'-0"

FIRST FLOOR 2883 SQ. FT.

DESIGN D2900
3,836 SQ. FT.
55,877 CU. FT.
3 BR, 2½ BA
FACES: N
SITE: LEVEL

A two-story sunspace adds drama to this contemporary home and provides solar heat to the upstairs and downstairs areas. The morning sun shines into the kitchen, breakfast room, and dining room. The adjacent deck is a perfect setting for morning meals in the sun and dinners in the shade. During the day the sun shines into the solarium through tall windows and three skylights. Excess heat rises naturally into the main living areas upstairs. Doors separating the sunspace from the rest of the house can be closed at night. Note the downstairs hot tub and sunken conversation lounge.

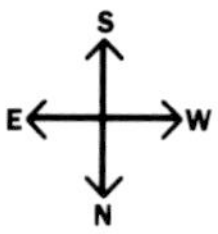

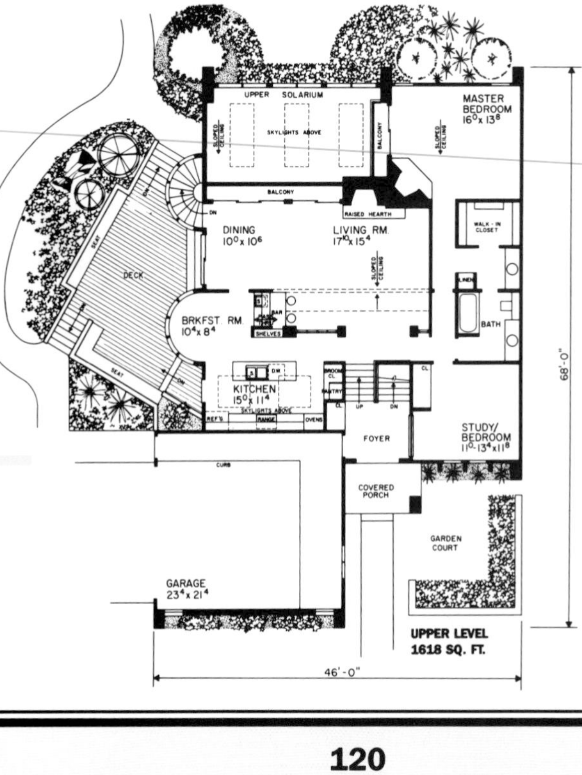

DESIGN D2827
3,364 SQ. FT.
41,370 CU. FT.
4 BR, 2 BA
FACES: N
SITE: LEVEL

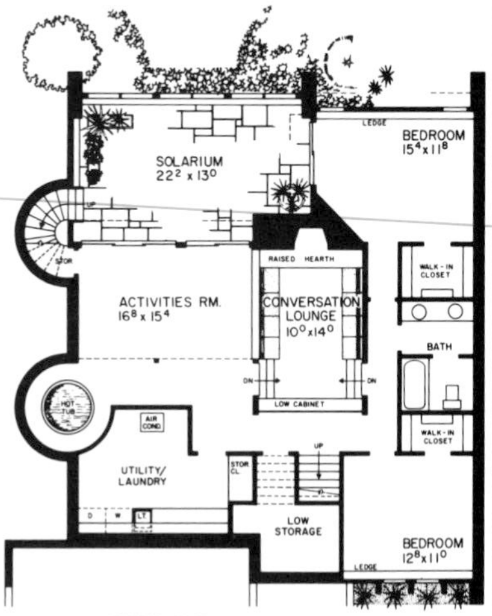

UPPER LEVEL
1618 SQ. FT.

LOWER LEVEL
1746 SQ. FT.

The tall and spacious sun-space is centrally situated so that it can provide solar heat, light, and gracious ambiance to both floors of this hand-some contemporary. The family room and excercise room also receive direct sun-shine during winter months. The exercise room has west windows as well. North win-dows in the front of the house bring indirect light into the master bedroom, living room, and foyer. Two of the upstairs bedrooms overlook the two-story sunspace, and the kitchen, breakfast room, and family room also have direct access to the heat and light captured in that space.

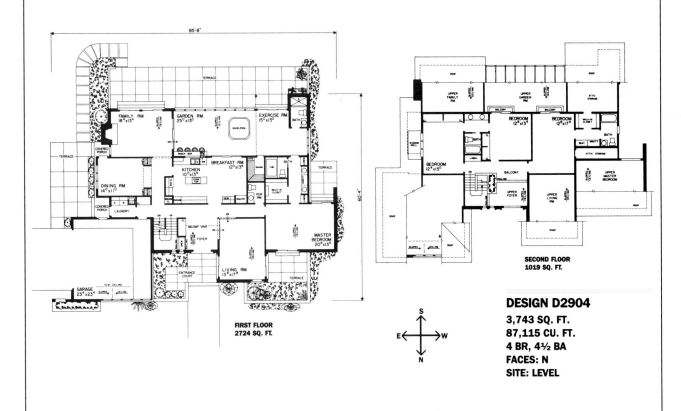

FIRST FLOOR
2724 SQ. FT.

SECOND FLOOR
1019 SQ. FT.

DESIGN D2904
3,743 SQ. FT.
87,115 CU. FT.
4 BR, 4½ BA
FACES: N
SITE: LEVEL

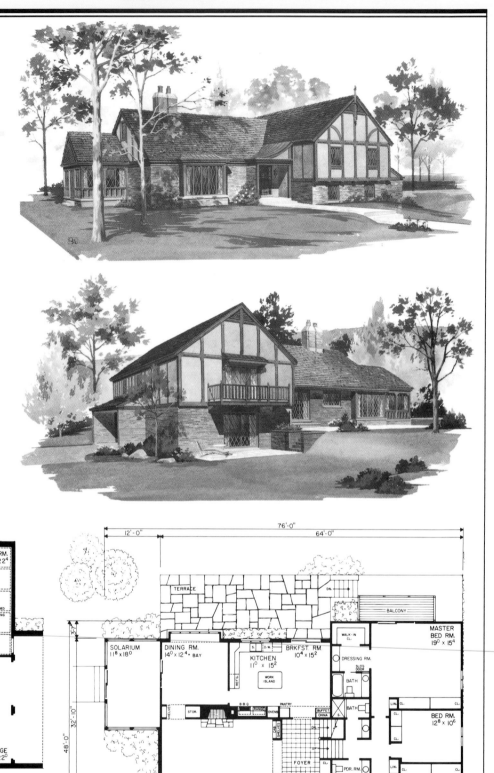

This charming Tudor features a sunspace on the east side and a large family room downstairs with access to a sunny terrace. The morning sun heats the sunspace quickly, warming the dining room and adjacent kitchen and living rooms as well. The bi-level floor plan helps distribute some of this heat to the upper rooms. The dining room, kitchen, breakfast room, and master bedroom also receive direct sunshine during winter. Three bedrooms receive afternoon sun. Note the bay windows in the dining room and living room, and the large basement.

DESIGN D2254

3,223 SQ. FT.
56,706 CU. FT.
4 BR, 3½ BA
FACES: N
SITE: SLOPES SW

This multi-level contemporary combines excellent solar exposure with convenient grouping of rooms. A sunspace and many windows on the south side let sunshine directly into the activities room, conversation area, dining room, family room, and two bedrooms throughout the day. Extra heat from the sunken sunspace flows upward into the adjacent rooms. The garage and sloping roof protect the north side of the home. Note the three skylights and the upstairs lounge overlooking both living room and front entry. Reversing this plan would bring morning sun into the kitchen area.

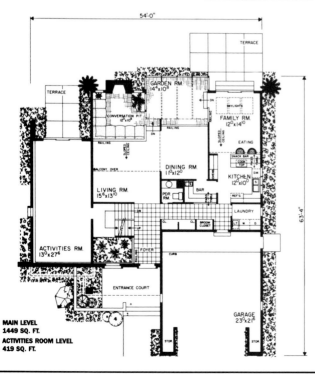

MASTER BEDROOM LEVEL
448 SQ. FT.

UPPER BEDROOM LEVEL
665 SQ. FT.

MAIN LEVEL
1449 SQ. FT.

ACTIVITIES ROOM LEVEL
419 SQ. FT.

DESIGN D2901
2,981 SQ. FT.
45,720 CU. FT.
3 BR, 2½ BA
FACES: N
SITE: SLOPES SE

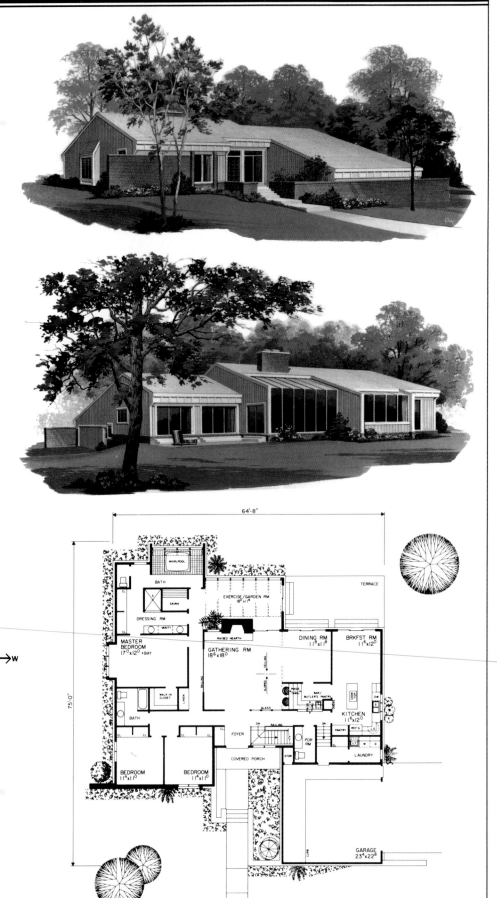

The large sunspace off the master bath makes an ideal exercise spa in this sunny contemporary. It can be opened to the gathering room to share the solar heat or closed off whenever desired. South windows bring more sunlight directly into the dining and breakfast rooms, and east windows brighten two of the bedrooms with morning light. Reversing this plan and adding a window to the side-wall of the breakfast room would bring morning light into the kitchen area and the end of the sunspace for quicker heating. Note the generous size and luxurious amenities of the master bath and the open plan of the central gathering room.

DESIGN D2873
2,838 SQ. FT.
58,960 CU. FT.
3 BR, 2½ BA
FACES: N
SITE: SLOPES N

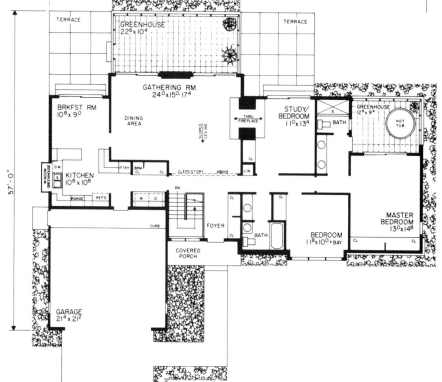

Two sunspaces and large windows at the back of this trim contemporary open all rooms except the north bedroom to direct sunlight. The kitchen receives direct sun in the morning and sunlight from the breakfast room during part of the day. The gathering room has access to the most solar heat through the large sunspace, which can be closed off at night. Note how the fireplace opens to both the gathering room and study. The master suite features a separate sunspace with hot tub, as well as closets along the north wall that could help buffer the room from cold winter blasts. Clerestory windows over the gathering room bring in additional daylight.

DESIGN D2886
2,127 SQ. FT.
34,986 CU. FT.
3 BR, 2 BA
FACES: N
SITE: LEVEL

Sunspaces to Brighten Work Areas

Large windows on the back and a sunspace on one side create many possibilities for living with the sun in this compact contemporary. In hot climates the back could be oriented to the north for maximum shading. In cooler climates the back should face south for daytime sunshine in the master bedroom, living room, dining room, and sunspace. Facing the back toward the southeast would bring even more sun to the sunspace. The plan could also be reversed so the kitchen and dining room receive morning sun and the sunspace heats up more quickly for daytime use. Note the secluded entry courtyard and the air-lock vestibule. Skylights brighten up the kitchen, laundry, and master bathroom, which also has its own whirlpool spa.

DESIGN D2902
1,848 SQ. FT.
40,723 CU. FT.
3 BR, 2½ BA
FACES: N or S
SITE: LEVEL

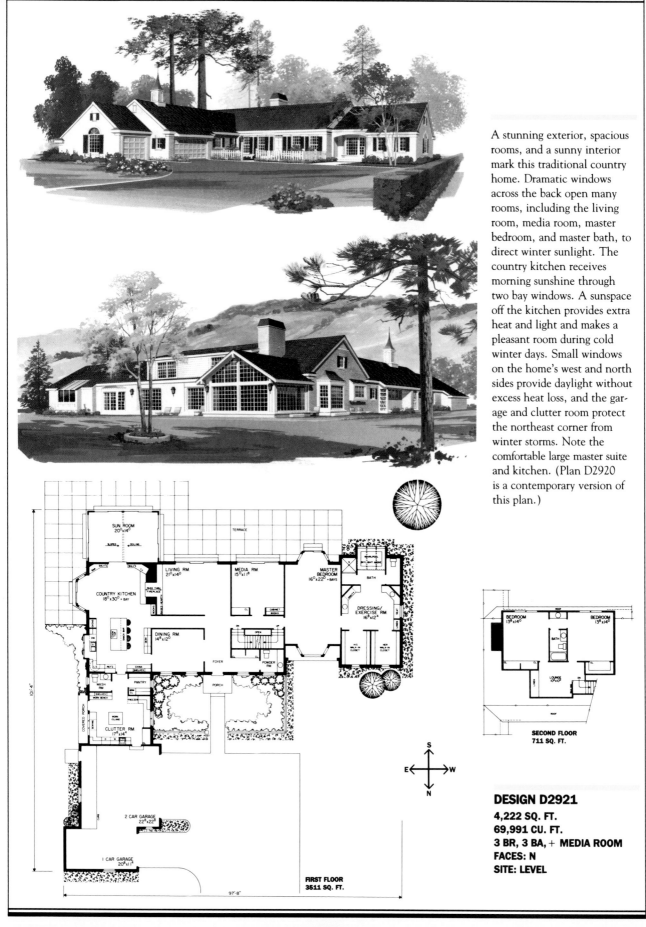

A stunning exterior, spacious rooms, and a sunny interior mark this traditional country home. Dramatic windows across the back open many rooms, including the living room, media room, master bedroom, and master bath, to direct winter sunlight. The country kitchen receives morning sunshine through two bay windows. A sunspace off the kitchen provides extra heat and light and makes a pleasant room during cold winter days. Small windows on the home's west and north sides provide daylight without excess heat loss, and the garage and clutter room protect the northeast corner from winter storms. Note the comfortable large master suite and kitchen. (Plan D2920 is a contemporary version of this plan.)

DESIGN D2921
4,222 SQ. FT.
69,991 CU. FT.
3 BR, 3 BA, + MEDIA ROOM
FACES: N
SITE: LEVEL

A handsome array of windows adds a modern touch to this traditional farmhouse design. The east-side sunspace floods the country kitchen with warmth and sunlight in the morning. During the day the generous window area on the south side lets the sun warm the kitchen, dining room, living room, master bedroom, and bathroom spa. Small windows on the west side limit the afternoon sunlight in one bedroom and two bathrooms. The media room and one bedroom on the north side are spared direct sunlight, and the clutter room has east windows for a sunny, early start on the laundry or other household projects. Note the two fireplaces and sloped ceilings.

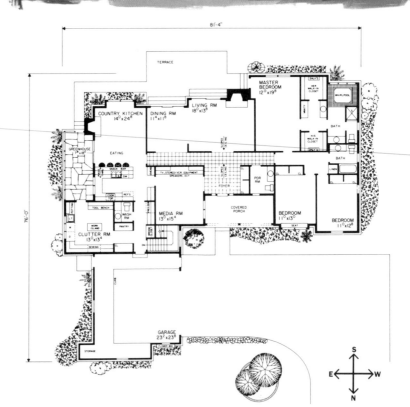

DESIGN D2880

2,907 SQ. FT.
60,850 CU. FT.
3 BR, 3 BA + MEDIA ROOM
FACES: N
SITE: LEVEL

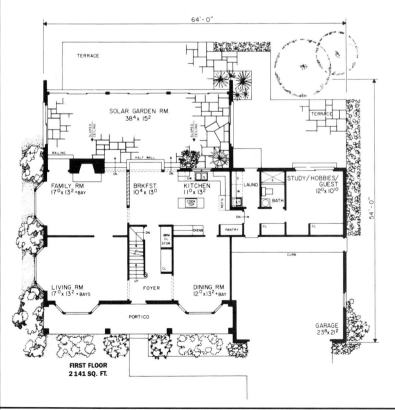

A sunken sunspace across the back of this Southern Colonial captures sunshine from early morning until late afternoon. The family room, breakfast nook, kitchen, and two upstairs bedrooms all receive heat and light from the sunlit space. The living room and dining room receive morning sunlight through bay windows, and an east window helps brighten the master bedroom in the morning. The late afternoon sun is restricted to the garage and a few small windows on the west side. Heat loss from the sunspace could be reduced by eliminating the skylights and restricting windows to the south wall. Note the balcony and large dressing area of the master suite.

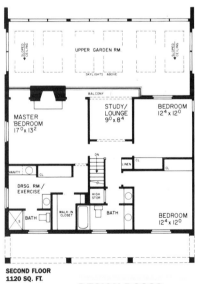

DESIGN D2839
3,261 SQ. FT.
58,925 CU. FT.
3 BR, 3 BA + STUDY
FACES: N
SITE: LEVEL

This charming Colonial features a spacious country kitchen with an attached sunspace in the back. The garage blocks sunlight from entering the sunspace until midday, but reversing the plan would solve this problem, exposing the greenhouse to direct sunshine from early morning until midafternoon. In the reverse plan, the garage would block late afternoon sun during summer months and would buffer the west side of the house against winter storms. In either orientation, the two upstairs bedrooms, the kitchen, and the dining room would receive direct sunshine during winter days, and the media room and living room would receive indirect north light. Note the south-facing bay window in the dining room and the large utility room off the garage.

DESIGN D2687

3,369 SQ. FT.
56,820 CU. FT.
4 BR, 2½ BA + STUDY
FACES: N
SITE: LEVEL

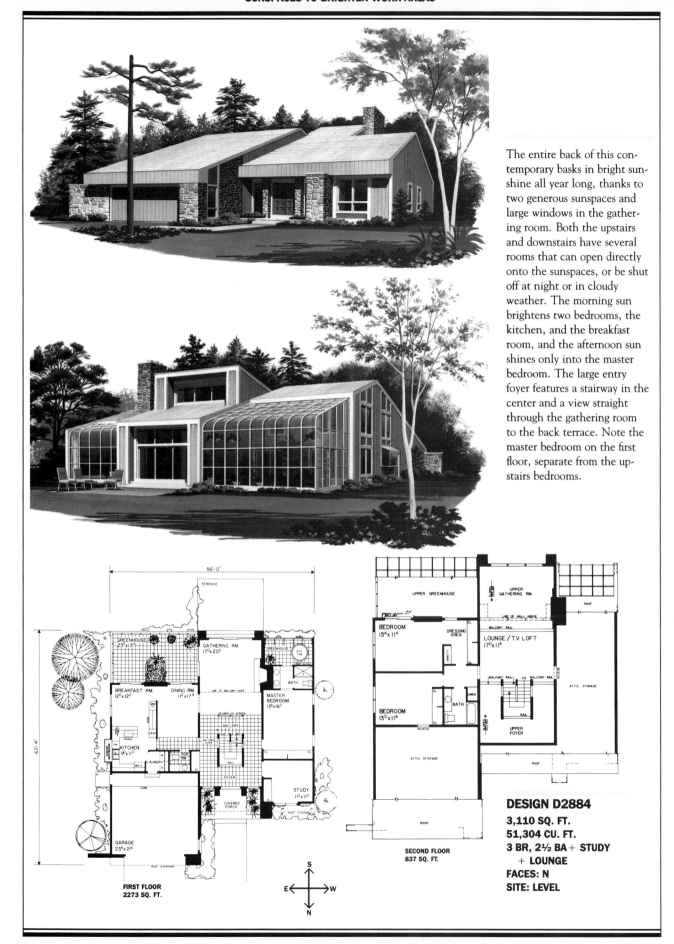

The entire back of this contemporary basks in bright sunshine all year long, thanks to two generous sunspaces and large windows in the gathering room. Both the upstairs and downstairs have several rooms that can open directly onto the sunspaces, or be shut off at night or in cloudy weather. The morning sun brightens two bedrooms, the kitchen, and the breakfast room, and the afternoon sun shines only into the master bedroom. The large entry foyer features a stairway in the center and a view straight through the gathering room to the back terrace. Note the master bedroom on the first floor, separate from the upstairs bedrooms.

DESIGN D2884
3,110 SQ. FT.
51,304 CU. FT.
3 BR, 2½ BA + STUDY
** + LOUNGE**
FACES: N
SITE: LEVEL

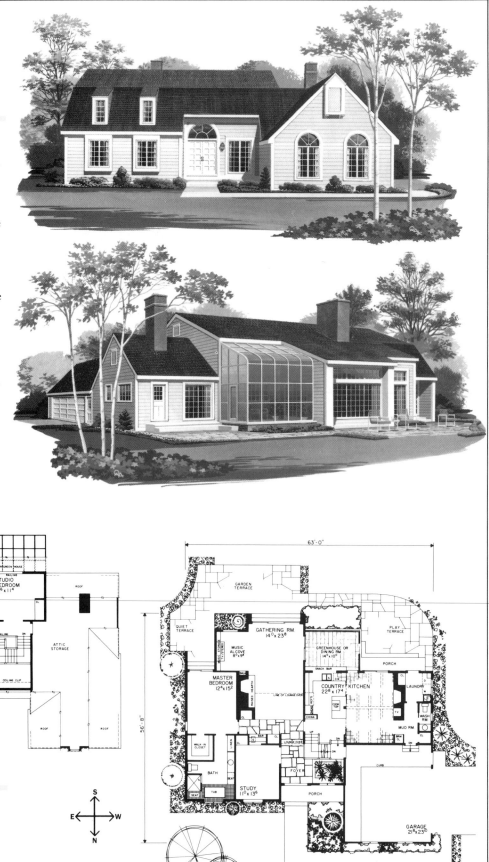

Country styling and a large window area along the back make this home warm and inviting. Three bedrooms have east windows for morning sunlight. Two bedrooms, the main gathering room, and the kitchen are flooded with sunlight during the day, partly through the dramatic sunspace. Extra heat easily finds its way upstairs — through the open balconies over the main gathering room and foyer and the studio overlooking the sunspace. The study has a window facing north for ideal working light, the garage protects the northwest corner of the home, and the attic adds bonus storage space.

DESIGN D2883

2,954 SQ. FT.
46,489 CU. FT.
4 BR, 2½ BA + STUDY
FACES: N
SITE: LEVEL

SECOND FLOOR
895 SQ. FT.

FIRST FLOOR
2059 SQ. FT.

This New England farmhouse features a sunspace and large windows on the south side for ideal solar gain. Sunlight in the morning enters east windows in the master bedroom, living room, and study. During the day the sun shines into the study, kitchen, sunspace, clutter room, and two bedrooms. A corner bedroom has windows on the west and north sides. The garage on the west side offers protection from hot afternoon sun. Note the three fireplaces, the special clutter room for household projects and storage, and the location of all bedrooms together on the second floor. The east and south windows of the study let in sunny morning warmth.

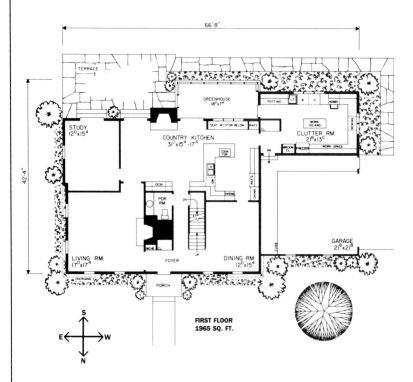

FIRST FLOOR
1965 SQ. FT.

SECOND FLOOR
1395 SQ. FT.

DESIGN D2692
3,360 SQ. FT.
53,581 CU. FT.
4 BR, 2½ BA + STUDY
FACES: N
SITE: LEVEL

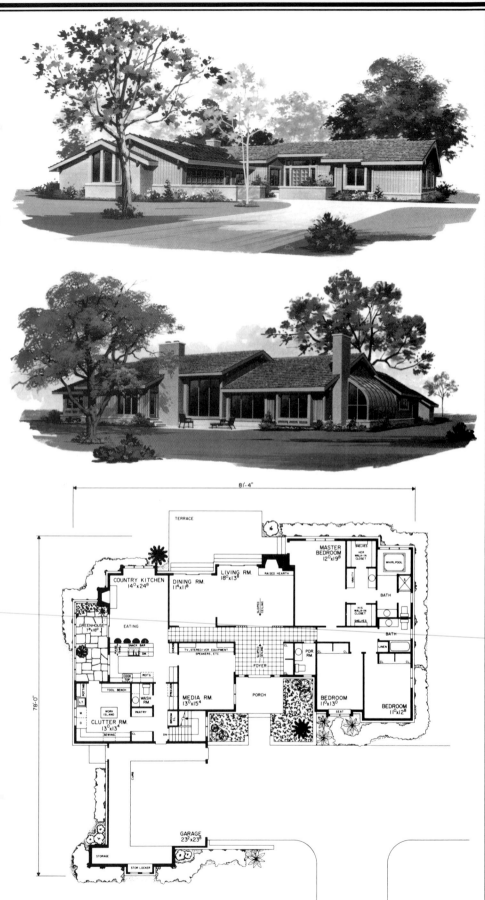

Living with the sun is a natural in this elegant contemporary. The sunspace on the east side captures early morning sunshine, warming the large country kitchen and providing a sunny spot for special breakfasts. During the day the winter sun pours into the kitchen, dining room, living room, master bedroom, and master bath. The west wall has few windows, reducing overheating from the late afternoon sun, and the garage helps protect the north side of the home. Note the special room for laundry and other household projects and the media room with only one window, ideal for TV viewing.

DESIGN D2915
2,907 SQ. FT.
60,850 CU. FT.
3 BR, 3 BA + MEDIA ROOM
FACES: N
SITE: LEVEL

Sunspaces for Outdoor Areas

Both the inside and outside of this classic Mediterranean home offer solar living at its finest. Large windows on the back of the home open the interior to winter sunshine. A deck and terrace create pleasant outdoor spaces for enjoying the sun or the shade. Most windows are on the south and north sides of the home, so summer overheating is kept to a minimum. The main living spaces, except for the kitchen, have south-facing windows. The master bedroom and breakfast area have north-facing windows for diffused light. The breakfast nook and kitchen have a view of the entry stairs.

DESIGN D2843
3,042 SQ. FT.
32,485 CU. FT.
4 BR, 3 BA
FACES: N
SITE: LEVEL or SLOPES S

LOWER LEVEL
1181 SQ. FT.

UPPER LEVEL
1861 SQ. FT.

The T-shape of this striking contemporary allows several rooms on both the upper and lower levels to face east and west where exposure to the morning and afternoon sun during the summer is desired. Early morning sun shines into the kitchen and breakfast nook, although it would be blocked during winter months by the walls of the main wing. The dining and family rooms have the same kind of exposure to the setting sun. Winter sun enters the study, three bedrooms, and the main gathering room, where tall windows allow the sunlight to reach far into the room. Note the balcony overlooking the main living space and the skylight above the balcony overlooking the main living space.

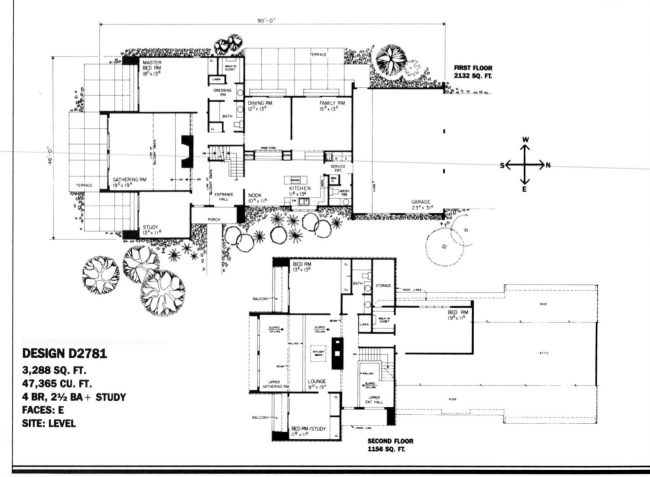

DESIGN D2781
3,288 SQ. FT.
47,365 CU. FT.
4 BR, 2½ BA + STUDY
FACES: E
SITE: LEVEL

The windows surrounding one end of this classic contemporary open the main living spaces to sunlight all day long. The living room, as well as three bedrooms and the study, receives morning sunshine. The living and dining areas receive the daytime winter sun, and the family room, master bedroom, kitchen, and eating nook receive the late afternoon sun. The lower level offers three separate rooms for maximum flexibility. Note how the family room opens onto the side terrace. Because the south-facing main living areas are elevated and protected by a balcony railing and planters, this home suits sites where the best solar orientation faces the street.

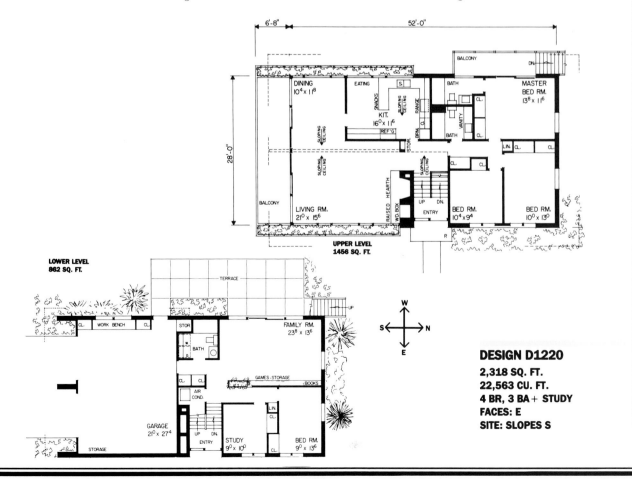

UPPER LEVEL
1456 SQ. FT.

LOWER LEVEL
862 SQ. FT.

DESIGN D1220
2,318 SQ. FT.
22,563 CU. FT.
4 BR, 3 BA + STUDY
FACES: E
SITE: SLOPES S

137

A covered porch lends charm to this cheerful country home. It extends along the north and east sides for cool, shady street-watching. The back of the home is open to the south for winter sunshine. The morning sun enters the dining room, living room, two upstairs bedrooms, and a side window of the breakfast room. The dining room, breakfast room, family room, and one upstairs bedroom receive sunshine throughout the rest of the day. The west wall has no windows and is protected by the garage and workshop. Note the two fireplaces, the curio shelves between the foyer and living room, and the pass-through between the kitchen and family room.

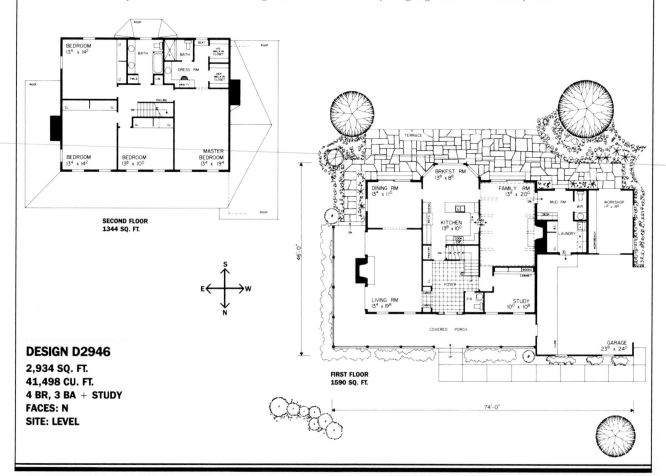

DESIGN D2946

2,934 SQ. FT.
41,498 CU. FT.
4 BR, 3 BA + STUDY
FACES: N
SITE: LEVEL

A family room with windows on both sides separates the bedroom wing from the public areas of this U-shaped Southwestern-style home. The covered porch behind the family room could be enclosed for a bonus sunspace or shortened to allow more sunshine into the home. The living room and dining room receive morning sun. The kitchen, breakfast room, and master bedroom receive sun during most of the day, and two bedrooms receive late afternoon sun. The unique entry court provides privacy as well as extra daylight for rooms surrounding it. Note the interestingly sloped ceilings of the living and dining rooms and the generous counter space in the laundry.

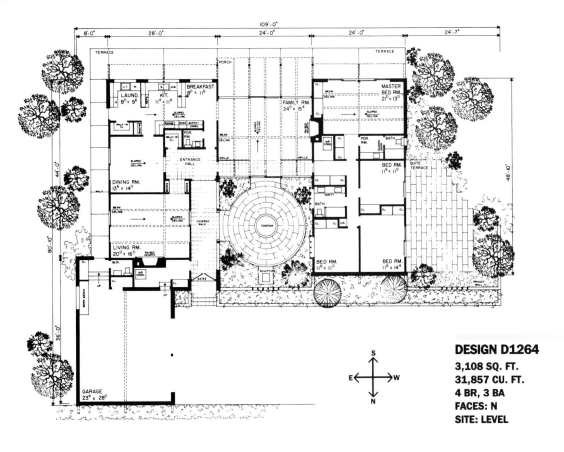

DESIGN D1264
3,108 SQ. FT.
31,857 CU. FT.
4 BR, 3 BA
FACES: N
SITE: LEVEL

Rich contemporary styling adds flair to this sun-filled home. All but two rooms have south-facing windows for maximum solar gain during winter months. Windows added to the east wall of the master bedroom would let in morning light, to complement the sunshine pouring in during the rest of the day. Balcony and roof overhangs for summer shading, limited window area on the west side, and the location of the garage on the northwest corner are other features that make this home ideal for solar living. Note the tall windows of the entry and the views from upstairs balconies into the dining room and kitchen.

SECOND FLOOR
1304 SQ. FT.

FIRST FLOOR
1643 SQ. FT.

DESIGN D2509
2,947 SQ. FT.
44,732 CU. FT.
4 BR, 2½ BA + STUDY
FACES: N
SITE: LEVEL

The graceful single-story entry of this hillside contemporary leads to two stories of sunny south windows in the back. All rooms except the kitchen have direct access to winter sunlight through south windows. The kitchen window faces the west sun, and a small window in the master bedroom receives the morning sun. The garage, low roof profile, and limited window area on the north side protect against winter storms. Direct access to the outdoors from every room enhances indoor-outdoor living, while fireplaces on both levels create cozy interiors. Note how the stairs from the lower level lead directly to the kitchen and laundry areas.

LOWER LEVEL
1558 SQ. FT.

MAIN LEVEL
1838 SQ. FT.

DESIGN D2583
3,396 SQ. FT.
29,400 CU. FT.
4 BR, 2½ BA + STUDY
FACES: N
SITE: SLOPES S

This home is especially suited for outdoor living in a warm climate, where outdoor spaces must be shaded. Facing the home toward the east minimizes the window areas exposed to direct sunlight. The south wall is protected by the garage, and only the glass doors of the master bedroom and the living room face that direction. The west wall has only two small windows. The majority of windows face north. The large side terrace is shaded by the house during most of the day, and the front entrance receives sun only in the morning. The master bedroom terrace offers full exposure to the sun. For cooler climates, orienting the home to the west gives the large window areas on the side full southern exposure. It also exposes the entrance court and tall windows of the family room and living room to late afternoon sun during the summer. The garage protects the north side of the home.

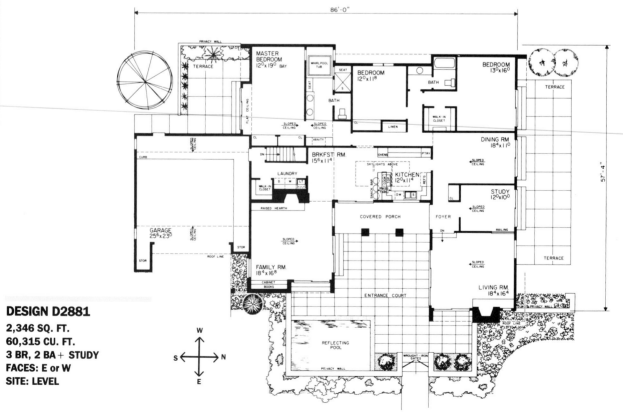

DESIGN D2881

2,346 SQ. FT.
60,315 CU. FT.
3 BR, 2 BA + STUDY
FACES: E or W
SITE: LEVEL

A formal court in the front distinguishes this Spanish-style home. It has large glass areas in both front and back, making it best suited for moderate or hot climates where heat loss is not a problem. Facing north, the home has the main living areas arrayed across the back for maximum solar heating during the winter. The kitchen, breakfast room, family room, activities room, and master bedroom become cheerful, sunny spaces for most of the day. The other bedrooms have north-facing windows for diffused daylight. This window area could be reduced for colder regions. The living room and dining room face north, which suits them for evening use or summer daytime use.

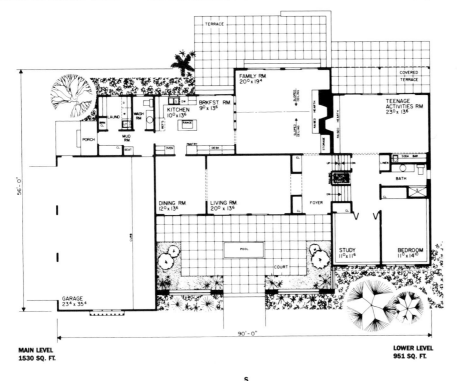

MAIN LEVEL
1530 SQ. FT.

LOWER LEVEL
951 SQ. FT.

UPPER LEVEL
984 SQ. FT.

DESIGN D2850
3,465 SQ. FT.
53,780 CU. FT.
4 BR, 3½ BA + STUDY
FACES: N
SITE: LEVEL

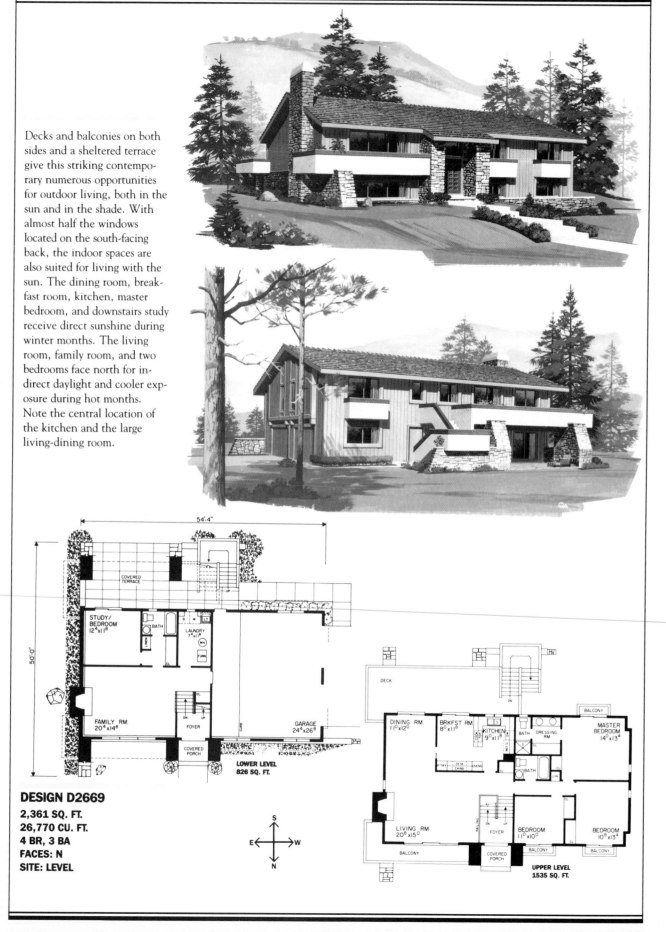

Decks and balconies on both sides and a sheltered terrace give this striking contemporary numerous opportunities for outdoor living, both in the sun and in the shade. With almost half the windows located on the south-facing back, the indoor spaces are also suited for living with the sun. The dining room, breakfast room, kitchen, master bedroom, and downstairs study receive direct sunshine during winter months. The living room, family room, and two bedrooms face north for indirect daylight and cooler exposure during hot months. Note the central location of the kitchen and the large living-dining room.

54'-4"

50'-0"

COVERED TERRACE

STUDY/ BEDROOM 12⁴x11⁸

BATH

LAUNDRY 7⁴x11⁸

FAMILY RM. 20⁴x14⁸

FOYER

GARAGE 24⁴x26⁸

COVERED PORCH

LOWER LEVEL
826 SQ. FT.

DESIGN D2669
2,361 SQ. FT.
26,770 CU. FT.
4 BR, 3 BA
FACES: N
SITE: LEVEL

DECK

DINING RM. 11⁰x12⁰

BRKFST RM. 8⁰x11⁸

KITCHEN 9⁰x11⁸

BATH

DRESSING RM

MASTER BEDROOM 14⁰x13⁴

BALCONY

PTRY

DESK CHINA

OVENS

BATH

LIVING RM. 20⁸x15⁰

FOYER

BEDROOM 11⁰x10⁰

BEDROOM 10⁸x13⁴

BALCONY

COVERED PORCH

BALCONY

BALCONY

UPPER LEVEL
1535 SQ. FT.

S

E   W

N

This Spanish-style home, with the protected front facing south for optimum cooling, fits right into a hot southwestern setting. (In other climates, face the front toward the north to let the sun into the family room, dining room, kitchen, and master bedroom.) The master bedroom has French doors that open onto a private deck, letting in the morning sun. Note the three-car garage, the separate eating area in the kitchen, and the cluster of bedrooms on the upper floor.

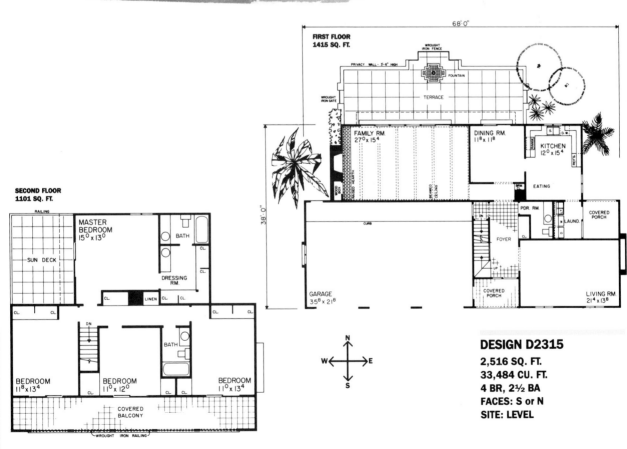

FIRST FLOOR
1415 SQ. FT.

68'-0"

38'-0"

WROUGHT IRON FENCE

PRIVACY WALL - 5'-6" HIGH

FOUNTAIN

WROUGHT IRON GATE

TERRACE

FAMILY RM.
27⁰ x 15⁴

DINING RM.
11⁸ x 11⁸

KITCHEN
12⁰ x 15⁴

WOOD BOX

RAISED HEARTH

BEAMED CEILING

EATING

GARAGE
35⁸ x 21⁸

CURB

PDR. RM.

LAUND.

COVERED PORCH

FOYER

UP

COVERED PORCH

LIVING RM.
21⁴ x 13⁸

SECOND FLOOR
1101 SQ. FT.

RAILING

MASTER BEDROOM
15⁰ x 13⁰

BATH

SUN DECK

CL.

DRESSING RM.

CL.

CL.

LINEN

CL.

CL.

CL.

CL.

DN

BATH

BEDROOM
11⁸ x 13⁴

BEDROOM
11⁰ x 12⁰

CL.

BEDROOM
11⁰ x 13⁸

CL.

CL.

COVERED BALCONY

WROUGHT IRON RAILING

N
W   E
S

DESIGN D2315

2,516 SQ. FT.
33,484 CU. FT.
4 BR, 2½ BA
FACES: S or N
SITE: LEVEL

With balconies and terraces on three sides of this handsome contemporary, almost every room has direct access to outdoor living. The inside of the house also opens up to the sun, with the master bedroom, two other bedrooms, activities room, kitchen, and dining room facing south to benefit from direct winter sunshine. The gathering room, family room, and study have north windows for indirect daylight. With windows on three walls, the large dining-gathering room upstairs and the family room downstairs are bright and cheery all day long.

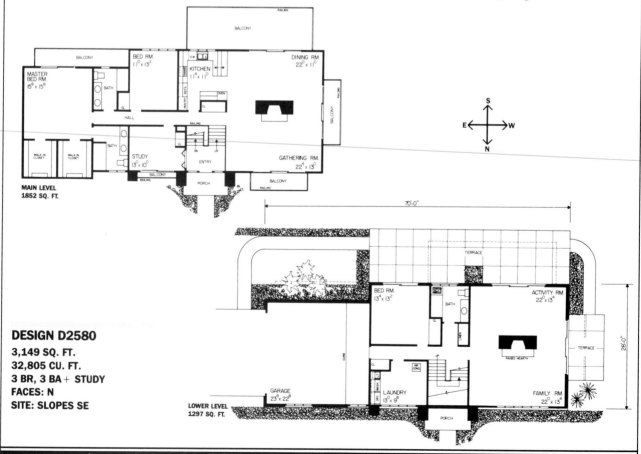

DESIGN D2580
3,149 SQ. FT.
32,805 CU. FT.
3 BR, 3 BA + STUDY
FACES: N
SITE: SLOPES SE

The two-story back of this hillside home admits direct sunlight into the main gathering room, dining room, master bedroom, and, depending on how far you extend the deck, downstairs rooms. The low profile and garage on the north side are ideal for conserving heat. The downstairs bedroom area, separate from the upstairs master bedroom, offers flexible space for casual living with direct access to the outdoors. Note the direct access from the garage to the entry. An east window in the kitchen nook brings morning sunlight to the breakfast table.

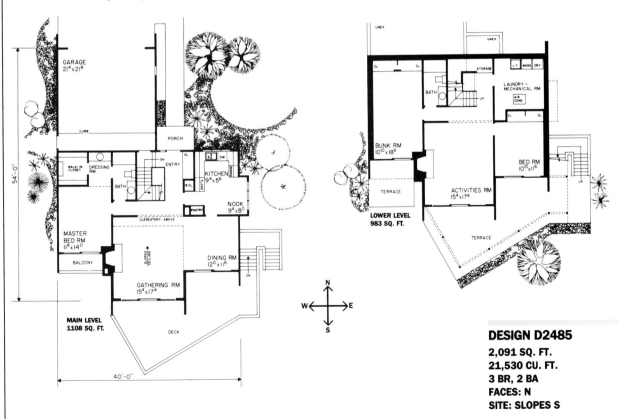

DESIGN D2485
2,091 SQ. FT.
21,530 CU. FT.
3 BR, 2 BA
FACES: N
SITE: SLOPES S

This Tudor home offers sunny living, both indoors and outdoors. Most of the windows are located in the back for ideal solar exposure. A spacious and convenient deck provides outdoor living in the sun, just a few steps from the kitchen and dining room. Because the deck faces south and is partially protected by the house, it can be used even on chilly days. On hot days, the downstairs terrace offers a cool, shady retreat. Indoors, the living room, dining room, kitchen, breakfast room, one bedroom, and downstairs family room all receive direct winter sunshine for most of the day. The downstairs study and two upstairs bedrooms have north-facing windows for indirect natural lighting. Note the convenient location of the kitchen and the separation of the bedrooms.

DECK

BEDROOM
12⁰ x 14⁴

BREAKFAST
12⁰ x 13⁶

DINING RM.
11⁰ x 13⁶

LIVING RM.
13⁰ x 19⁰ + BAY

KITCHEN
10⁰ x 13⁶

OVEN PNTRY

CL

CL

LINEN

BRM CL

BATH

LAUNDRY

DN   UP

CL

WALK-IN CLOSET

BATH

BEDROOM
12⁰ x 12⁰

FOYER

MASTER BEDROOM
16⁰ x 12⁰

COVERED PORCH

UPPER LEVEL
1882 SQ. FT.

62'-0"

COVERED   TERRACE

FAMILY RM.
24⁸ x 13⁶

HOBBIES/SHOP
12⁰ x 10⁶

FURN

BOOKS DESK

7'-4"

28'-8"

41'-8"

GARAGE
20⁰ x 27⁴

STORAGE

DN   UP

BATH

WALK-IN CLOSET

FOYER

LINEN

BEDROOM/STUDY
14⁴ x 12¹⁰

COVERED PORCH

5'-8"

LOWER LEVEL
1168 SQ. FT.

DESIGN D2844
3,050 SQ. FT.
37,860 CU. FT.
4 BR, 3 BA
FACES: N
SITE: LEVEL or SLOPES SE

S
E — W
N

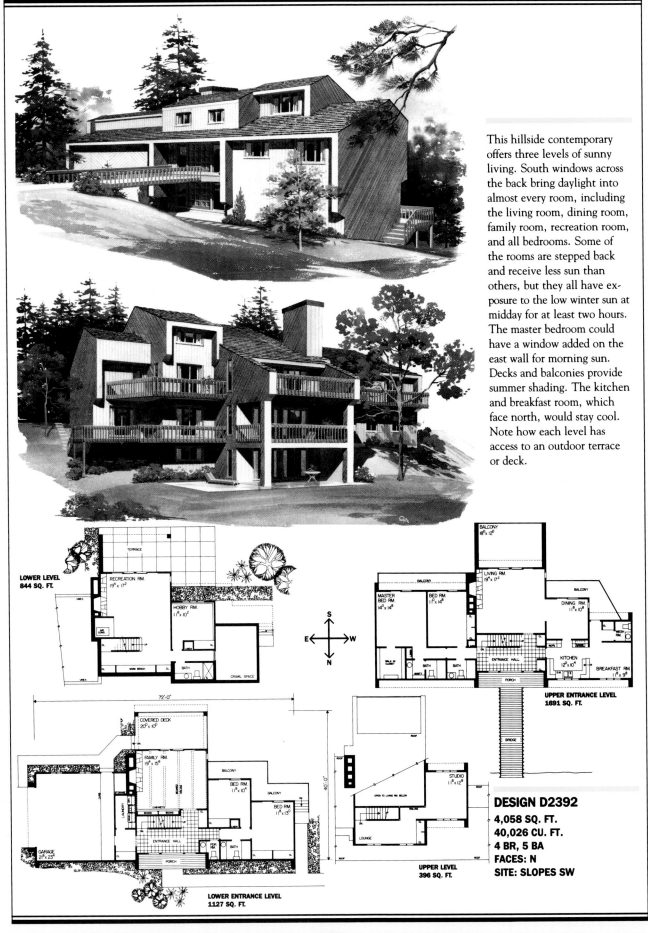

This hillside contemporary offers three levels of sunny living. South windows across the back bring daylight into almost every room, including the living room, dining room, family room, recreation room, and all bedrooms. Some of the rooms are stepped back and receive less sun than others, but they all have exposure to the low winter sun at midday for at least two hours. The master bedroom could have a window added on the east wall for morning sun. Decks and balconies provide summer shading. The kitchen and breakfast room, which face north, would stay cool. Note how each level has access to an outdoor terrace or deck.

LOWER LEVEL
844 SQ. FT.

TERRACE

RECREATION RM.
19⁴ x 17²

HOBBY RM.
11⁸ x 10²

WORK BENCH

BATH

CRAWL SPACE

UPPER ENTRANCE LEVEL
1691 SQ. FT.

BALCONY
18⁴ x 12⁰

LIVING RM.
19⁴ x 17²

BALCONY

BALCONY

MASTER BED RM.
14⁰ x 14⁸

BED RM.
11⁴ x 14⁸

DINING RM.
11⁸ x 10⁸

WALK IN CLOSET

BATH

BATH

ENTRANCE HALL

KITCHEN
12⁰ x 10⁴

BREAKFAST RM.
11⁸ x 9⁸

WASH RM.

PORCH

BRIDGE

72'-0"

COVERED DECK
20⁰ x 10⁰

FAMILY RM.
19⁴ x 15⁸

BALCONY

BED RM.
11⁸ x 10⁴

BALCONY

BED RM.
11⁸ x 13⁰

40'-0"

GARAGE
21⁸ x 23⁴

LAUNDRY

CABINETS

BOOKS

BOOKS

ENTRANCE HALL

BATH

PORCH

LOWER ENTRANCE LEVEL
1127 SQ. FT.

ROOF

ROOF

STUDIO
11⁸ x 12⁸

ROOF

OPEN TO LIVING RM. BELOW

LOUNGE

ROOF

UPPER LEVEL
396 SQ. FT.

DESIGN D2392
4,058 SQ. FT.
40,026 CU. FT.
4 BR, 5 BA
FACES: N
SITE: SLOPES SW

149

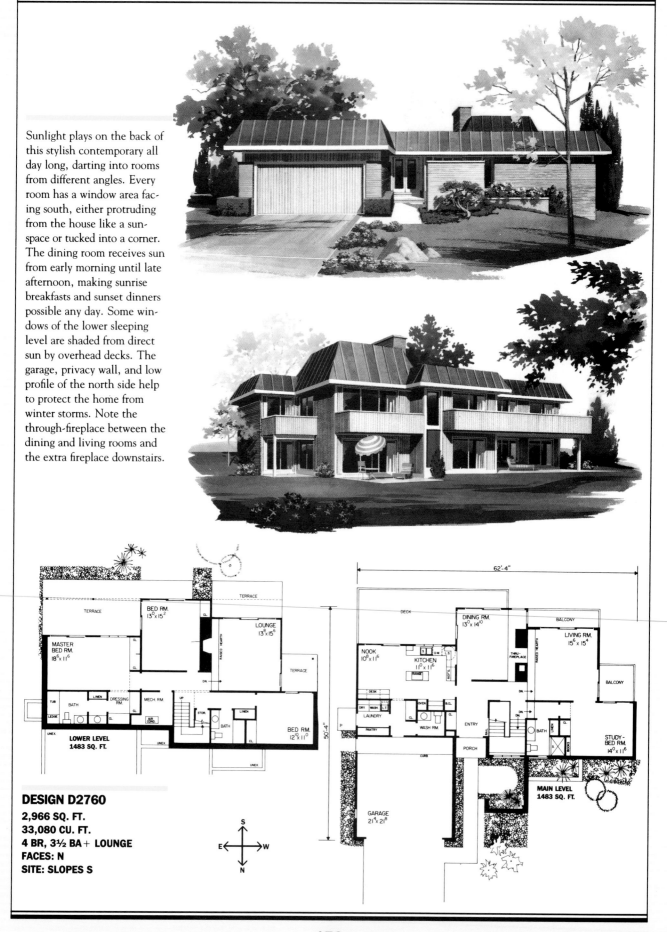

Sunlight plays on the back of this stylish contemporary all day long, darting into rooms from different angles. Every room has a window area facing south, either protruding from the house like a sunspace or tucked into a corner. The dining room receives sun from early morning until late afternoon, making sunrise breakfasts and sunset dinners possible any day. Some windows of the lower sleeping level are shaded from direct sun by overhead decks. The garage, privacy wall, and low profile of the north side help to protect the home from winter storms. Note the through-fireplace between the dining and living rooms and the extra fireplace downstairs.

DESIGN D2760
2,966 SQ. FT.
33,080 CU. FT.
4 BR, 3½ BA + LOUNGE
FACES: N
SITE: SLOPES S

150

Controlling the Sun

At certain times of the year, certain times of day, or in certain climates it is difficult to enjoy the sun without the benefit of some shading. The plans in this section show some ways to control the sun without blocking it from the house or allowing direct gain through south-facing windows.

COVERED PORCHES. The first group of plans, Covered Porches, features covered outdoor areas. These classic porch designs offer shady retreats within steps of your doorway, where you can entertain visitors, read, let the children play, or relax and watch the world go by. The porch locations differ, allowing you to choose which time of day and on which side of the home you have outdoor shade. Most of the porches can be screened to keep pests out.

ROOF GABLES AND OVERHANGS. The second section of plans, Roof Gables and Overhangs, features homes with broad roof overhangs that shade windows during hot summer months. Some of the overhangs are on the south side of the home, others on the east or west side. Although such overhangs will not provide full shade all year

round and may need to be augmented by other shading devices, they offer significant heat reduction. Some of the plans feature trellises and roof openings that filter the sunshine, reducing the sun that enters through windows.

SKYLIGHTS AND CLERESTORIES. The third section of plans, Skylights and Clerestories, shows how glazed overhead openings can bring sunshine into the interior areas of a home. They make it possible to enjoy living with the sun even when site conditions block direct solar gain through other windows. Although skylights do not admit as much winter sunshine as windows, they still create dramatic effects, provide light, and admit some heat.

DESIGNING WITH SOLAR COLLECTORS. The fourth section, Designing with Solar Collectors, includes three active solar designs that use solar collectors on the roof for heating. These are not strictly "passive solar" designs, but they provide a method of gathering heat where large areas of south-facing windows are not feasible. Solar collectors installed on an expansive roof area can provide a large percentage of the energy required for heating.

Covered Porches

This handsome traditional home features covered porches on the front and back, making it possible to orient the home to the north or south and still keep it cool. With either orientation, the garage and clutter room protect one side of the house from the low sun. An orientation to the east or west is even possible, although this exposes the two long sides to the hottest sun. Note the separate library and the windows at opposite ends of the kitchen.

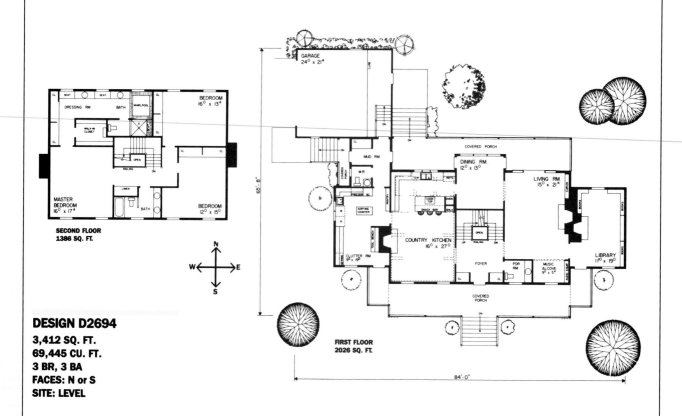

SECOND FLOOR
1386 SQ. FT.

FIRST FLOOR
2026 SQ. FT.

DESIGN D2694
3,412 SQ. FT.
69,445 CU. FT.
3 BR, 3 BA
FACES: N or S
SITE: LEVEL

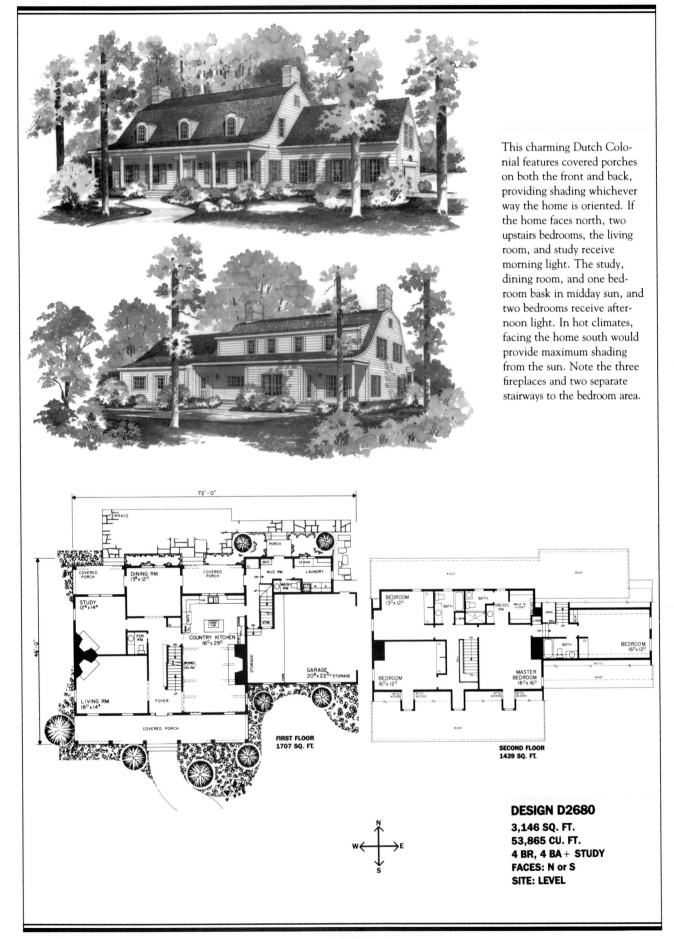

This charming Dutch Colonial features covered porches on both the front and back, providing shading whichever way the home is oriented. If the home faces north, two upstairs bedrooms, the living room, and study receive morning light. The study, dining room, and one bedroom bask in midday sun, and two bedrooms receive afternoon light. In hot climates, facing the home south would provide maximum shading from the sun. Note the three fireplaces and two separate stairways to the bedroom area.

FIRST FLOOR
1707 SQ. FT.

SECOND FLOOR
1439 SQ. FT.

DESIGN D2680
3,146 SQ. FT.
53,865 CU. FT.
4 BR, 4 BA+ STUDY
FACES: N or S
SITE: LEVEL

This delightful farmhouse is perfect for lots where morning sunlight is blocked or privacy favors few windows facing east. Instead, sunlight pours into the family room, breakfast room, kitchen, dining room, and two bedrooms during the middle of the day. The living room receives sun only in the summer months in the late afternoon. Orienting the back of the house toward the southeast will bring sunlight into the main living spaces earlier in the day and make it possible to watch sunsets from the living room year-round. Note the bonus space in the attic.

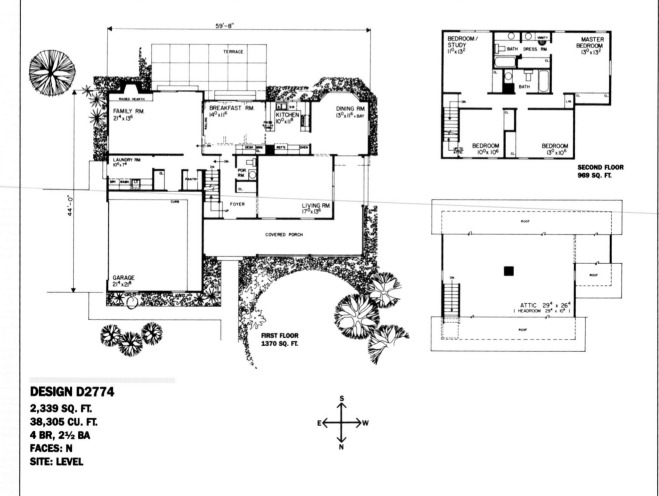

DESIGN D2774
2,339 SQ. FT.
38,305 CU. FT.
4 BR, 2½ BA
FACES: N
SITE: LEVEL

Shaded porches protect windows from excess sun and provide a pleasant outdoor retreat, making this gracious Colonial especially suitable for hot climates. Orienting the front to the north would bring morning sun into the east windows and leave only two windows facing west. The garage would provide additional shading on the west side. Note how the kitchen spans the entire house and the entry foyer extends to the back of the house.

DESIGN D2686

3,224 SQ. FT.
57,345 CU. FT.
3 BR, 2½ BA
FACES: N or S
SITE: LEVEL

With its covered porch and balcony and spacious country kitchen, this traditional home offers leisure living at its best. There is the option of orienting the home to the north or south, depending on whether you need to get into the sun or out of the sun. If the front faces north, the windows of the back admit direct sunshine into the dining room, kitchen, and two upstairs bedrooms. If the front faces south, it is shaded from direct sun by the balcony and porch roof, and the large window area of the back would face north, away from the sun.

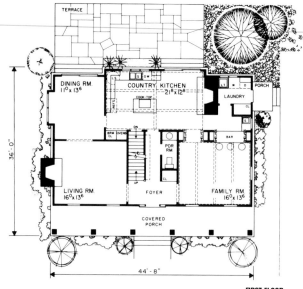

SECOND FLOOR
1262 SQ. FT.

DESIGN D2664
2,570 SQ. FT.
49,215 CU. FT.
4 BR, 2½ BA
FACES: N or S
SITE: LEVEL

FIRST FLOOR
1308 SQ. FT.

The spacious porch and the room arrangement of this appealing home combine to offer cool and comfortable living in hot weather. The porch wraps around the north half of the home, providing a retreat from the hot sun of late summer afternoons. It also protects the rooms on the west and north sides from the sun. The kitchen, dining room, living room, and two upstairs bedrooms all have north exposures. The back of the house faces south, bringing direct sunshine into the family room, study, and one upstairs bedroom during the winter. The garage and laundry protect the east side of the house. Note the location of the study, in a quiet corner of the house.

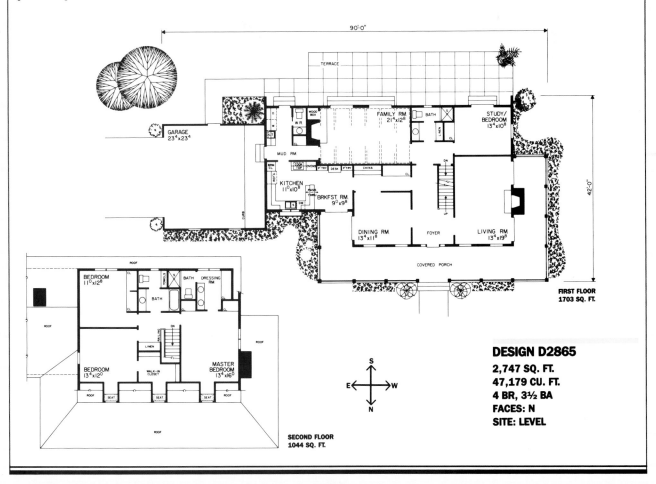

DESIGN D2865
2,747 SQ. FT.
47,179 CU. FT.
4 BR, 3½ BA
FACES: N
SITE: LEVEL

This elegant home, based on designs typical of eighteenth-century Charleston, South Carolina, is suited for a warm climate where rooms need to be restricted in their exposure to the sun. The tiered balconies protect the south-facing front from direct sunlight, and the narrow ends limit the amount of wall exposed to the hot sun from the east and west. These sides should be shaded by trees or other devices. Note that the main part of the house is only one room wide; such designs were referred to as "single houses." The wing with garage, kitchen, and bedroom is an added feature, not typical of the traditional design.

DESIGN D2660
4,448 SQ. FT.
57,440 CU. FT.
5 BR, 5 BA + STUDY
FACES: S
SITE: LEVEL

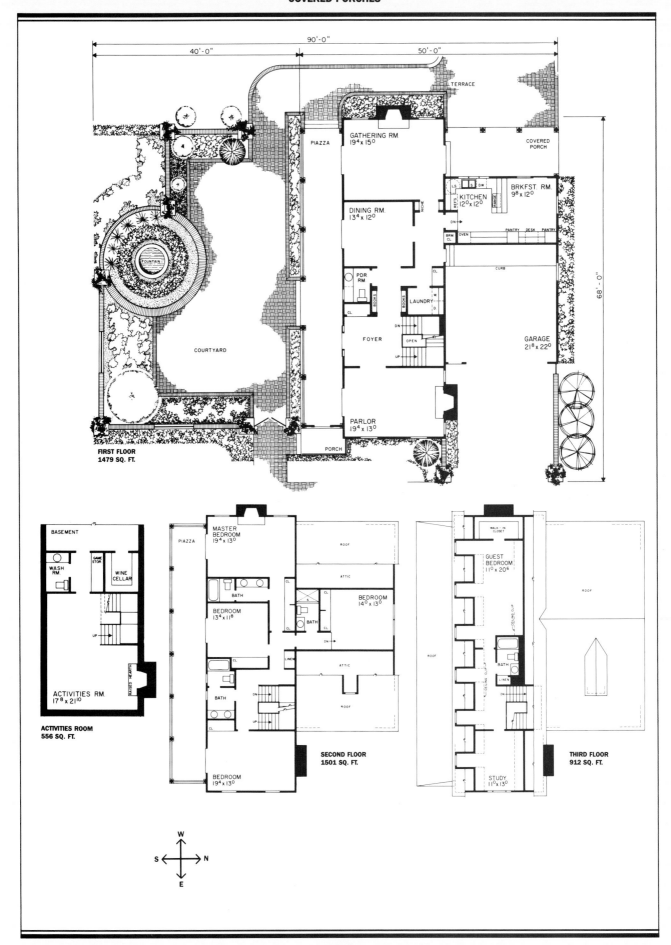

90'-0"
40'-0"
50'-0"

68'-0"

TERRACE

PIAZZA

GATHERING RM.
19⁴ x 15⁰

COVERED
PORCH

BRKFST. RM.
9⁸ x 12⁰

KITCHEN
12⁰ x 12⁰

DINING RM.
13⁴ x 12⁰

NICHE

OVEN PANTRY DESK PANTRY

BRM
CL.

CURB

PDR
RM

CL

BOOKS

BOOKS

LAUNDRY

FOUNTAIN

CL

GARAGE
21⁸ x 22⁰

FOYER

OPEN

DN

UP

COURTYARD

PARLOR
19⁴ x 13⁰

PORCH

**FIRST FLOOR
1479 SQ. FT.**

BASEMENT

GAME
STOR

WASH
RM.

WINE
CELLAR

PIAZZA

MASTER
BEDROOM
19⁴ x 13⁰

ROOF

WALK - IN
CLOSET

ATTIC

GUEST
BEDROOM
11⁰ x 20⁶

ROOF

BATH

CL

CL

BEDROOM
14⁰ x 13⁰

BEDROOM
13⁴ x 11⁸

BATH

S

BATH

LINEN

ROOF

BATH

LINEN

UP

RAISED HEARTH

ACTIVITIES RM.
17⁸ x 21¹⁰

LINEN

ATTIC

DN

ROOF

DN

BATH

CL

BEDROOM
19⁴ x 13⁰

UP

STUDY
11⁰ x 13⁰

**ACTIVITIES ROOM
556 SQ. FT.**

**SECOND FLOOR
1501 SQ. FT.**

**THIRD FLOOR
912 SQ. FT.**

W
S   N
E

This charming traditional home offers limited exposure to the sun in both the front and back. If the home faces north, the back has only a few south-facing windows. The west side is protected by the garage and the east side has only four small windows. If the home faces south, the front has small windows in the dormers upstairs and a porch shading the downstairs windows. All these features add up to a comfortable home for warm climates where protection from the sun is needed.

SECOND FLOOR
1091 SQ. FT.

WALK-IN CLOSET

DRESSING RM. SHELVES

BATH

BED RM 11⁴ x 10⁰

BATH

CL CL

ROOF

MASTER BED RM 18⁰ x 14¹⁰

DN SHELVES LINEN SHELVES

BED RM 17⁰ x 12⁶

S
E ⊕ W
N

DESIGN D2650
2,542 SQ. FT.
43,555 CU. FT.
3 BR, 2½ BA + STUDY
FACES: N or S
SITE: LEVEL

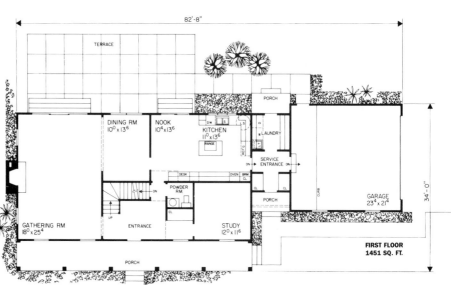

82'-8"

TERRACE

DINING RM 10⁰ x 13⁶

NOOK 10⁴ x 13⁶

KITCHEN 11⁰ x 13⁶ RANGE

PORCH

LAUNDRY

SERVICE ENTRANCE

GARAGE 23⁴ x 21⁴

34'-0"

DESK OVEN BRM

POWDER RM CL

GATHERING RM 18⁰ x 25⁴

UP DN ENTRANCE

STUDY 12⁰ x 11⁶

PORCH

PORCH

FIRST FLOOR
1451 SQ. FT.

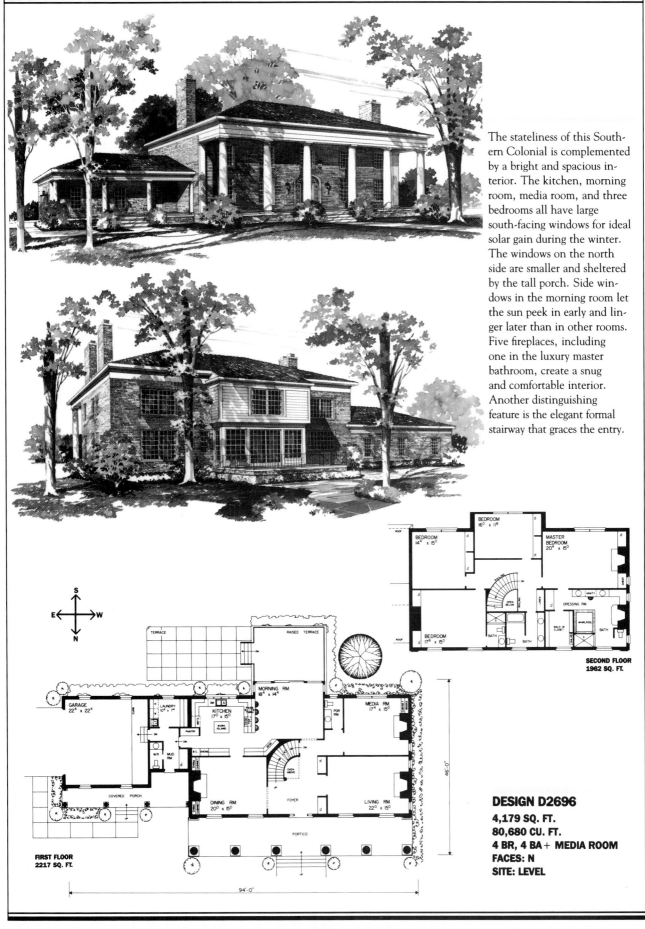

The stateliness of this Southern Colonial is complemented by a bright and spacious interior. The kitchen, morning room, media room, and three bedrooms all have large south-facing windows for ideal solar gain during the winter. The windows on the north side are smaller and sheltered by the tall porch. Side windows in the morning room let the sun peek in early and linger later than in other rooms. Five fireplaces, including one in the luxury master bathroom, create a snug and comfortable interior. Another distinguishing feature is the elegant formal stairway that graces the entry.

SECOND FLOOR
1962 SQ. FT.

FIRST FLOOR
2217 SQ. FT.

DESIGN D2696
4,179 SQ. FT.
80,680 CU. FT.
4 BR, 4 BA + MEDIA ROOM
FACES: N
SITE: LEVEL

Roof Gables and Overhangs

The back of this Spanish-style home has two levels of south-facing windows for direct solar heating in all the main living spaces. The family room, kitchen, dining room, living room, master bedroom, and downstairs rooms receive winter sunshine most of the day. Two bedrooms have east windows for morning sun. The west side has no windows, and the north side has windows for the study and one bathroom. The deck provides shade for the downstairs windows, creating a cool summer retreat complete with its own kitchen. Both kitchens are conveniently close to the stairway, which also has easy access to the children's bedrooms.

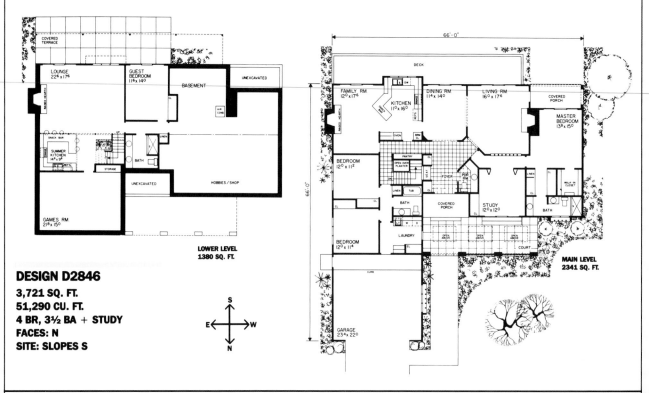

COVERED TERRACE

LOUNGE 22⁶ x 17⁶

GUEST BEDROOM 11⁶ x 14⁰

BASEMENT

UNEXCAVATED

AIR COND

SNACK BAR

SUMMER KITCHEN 14⁴ x 9⁶

LINEN

BATH

STORAGE

UNEXCAVATED

HOBBIES / SHOP

GAMES RM 21⁸ x 15⁰

**LOWER LEVEL
1380 SQ. FT.**

66'-0"

DECK

FAMILY RM 12⁰ x 17⁶

KITCHEN 11⁰ x 16⁰

DINING RM 11⁴ x 14⁰

LIVING RM 16⁰ x 17⁶

COVERED PORCH

MASTER BEDROOM 13⁸ x 15⁰

OVEN

BRM

PANTRY

OPEN OVER PLANTER

BEDROOM 12⁰ x 11²

FOYER

POR

LINEN

WALK-IN CLOSET

66'-0"

LINEN TUB

BATH

COVERED PORCH

STUDY 12⁰ x 12⁰

BATH

BEDROOM 12⁰ x 11⁴

LAUNDRY

OPEN ABOVE

OPEN ABOVE

OPEN ABOVE

COURT

CURB

GARAGE 23⁴ x 22⁰

**MAIN LEVEL
2341 SQ. FT.**

**DESIGN D2846
3,721 SQ. FT.
51,290 CU. FT.
4 BR, 3½ BA + STUDY
FACES: N
SITE: SLOPES S**

S
E W
N

The long shape of this contemporary home is ideal for solar living. The living room receives morning and daytime sun. The dining room and kitchen-nook receive sun throughout the winter, and the living room and master bedroom receive some winter sun beneath the porch overhangs. These overhangs help with summer cooling and create sheltered access between garage and kitchen; this area could be enclosed for a sunspace. The separate bedroom area has two bathrooms, and the two smaller bedrooms could be joined for a play and sleeping area. The sloped ceiling and expansive glass in the living room create a spacious feeling. The dining-living room offers outdoor access.

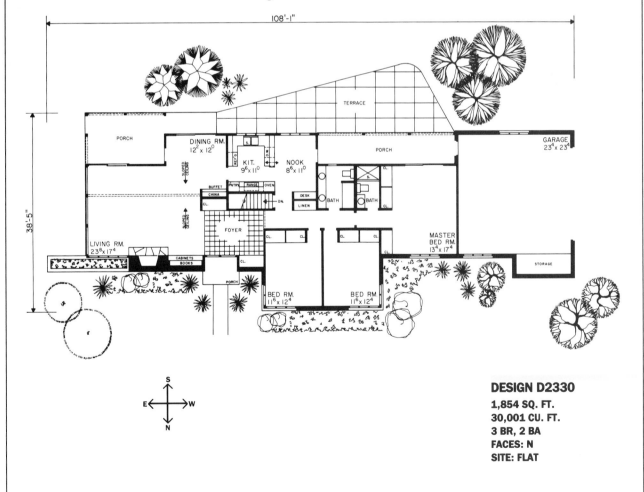

DESIGN D2330
1,854 SQ. FT.
30,001 CU. FT.
3 BR, 2 BA
FACES: N
SITE: FLAT

This Spanish-inspired home has large window areas in the back, as well as an enclosed porch for outdoor living in the shade. The sides of the house, with few windows, are protected from overheating. The master bedroom receives sun in midmorning, but it is shaded by the gathering room wall later. The gathering room and dining room receive sun throughout most of the day in the winter. Roof vents over the breakfast room window bring daylight into the covered entry porch and the kitchen. The gathering room, dining room, and covered dining porch can be opened to each other for entertaining. (Plan D2802 is a Tudor version of this plan, and D2803 is a contemporary version.)

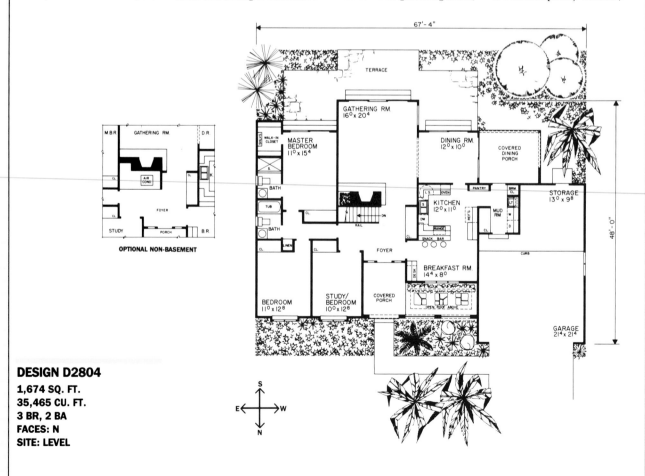

DESIGN D2804
1,674 SQ. FT.
35,465 CU. FT.
3 BR, 2 BA
FACES: N
SITE: LEVEL

Dramatic indoor spaces and controlled exposure to the sun distinguish this Mediterranean-style home. The south side has windows in the master bedroom, family room, breakfast room, and kitchen for direct winter sunshine, although the family room does not receive sun until midday. The west-facing windows of the master bedroom are shaded by a terrace trellis similar to the one at the entrance. The garage and utility spaces protect the west wall, and the east side has only one window for morning sun in one of the bedrooms. An atrium lets daylight into the interior of the house. (Skylight shades can be drawn to keep direct sun out of the atrium when necessary.) Note the clear separation of the bedroom and family areas from the formal areas.

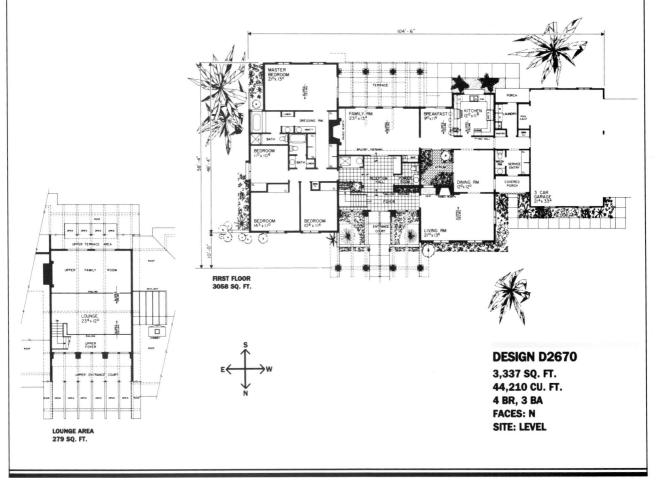

LOUNGE AREA
279 SQ. FT.

FIRST FLOOR
3058 SQ. FT.

DESIGN D2670
3,337 SQ. FT.
44,210 CU. FT.
4 BR, 3 BA
FACES: N
SITE: LEVEL

The master bedroom, study, gathering room, and dining room of this clean-lined contemporary all have south-facing windows for midday sunshine. A window added to the east wall of the master bedroom would give it morning light. Because it has no west-facing windows, the dining room on the west side is protected from afternoon overheating. The garage in the northwest corner acts as a buffer against winter storms. The kitchen looks out on the private entry court, and the breakfast nook has direct access to the court. Notice how the three main zones — sleeping rooms, work areas, public spaces — radiate from the entry foyer for effortless traffic flow.

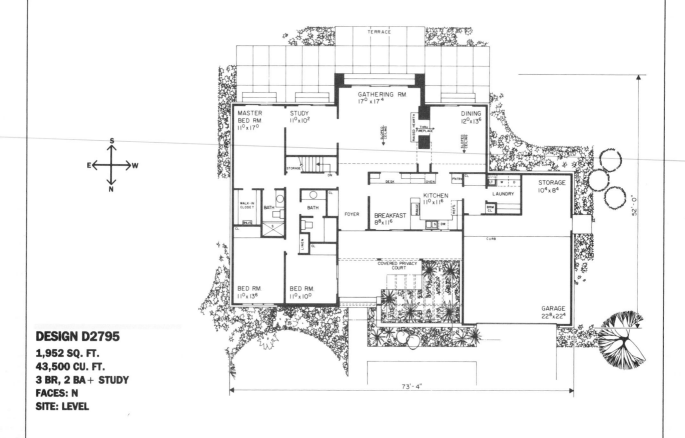

DESIGN D2795
1,952 SQ. FT.
43,500 CU. FT.
3 BR, 2 BA + STUDY
FACES: N
SITE: LEVEL

The soaring gable windows featured on the front of this dramatic contemporary are shaded by wide roof overhangs, making it possible to orient the front either to the south or the north. This home is ideal where views and hot weather favor a north orientation because the front has as much window area as the back. The roof overhangs, trellis over the dining room windows, and garage provide shade. Note the few windows on the sides of the home where low sun might otherwise cause overheating. If the back faces south, the main living areas of the home would receive direct sun in the winter. A gable similar to the ones in front shades the high windows of the gathering room.

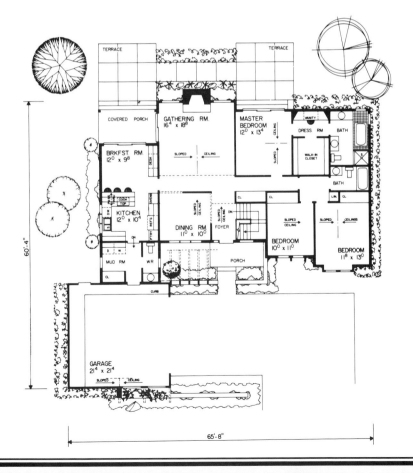

DESIGN D2917

1,813 SQ. FT.
39,765 CU. FT.
3 BR, 2½ BA
FACES: N or S
SITE: LEVEL

This contemporary with a tropical flair has few windows and wide overhangs in the front, making it appropriate for both hot and cool climates. Face it south in hot climates so that the back opens to the outdoors without being exposed to the harsh sun. Face it north in moderate or cool climates for maximum solar gain. In this case, the kitchen would receive sun in the morning, and the family room, living room, and master bedroom would be sunny throughout the day. Only one bedroom would have windows facing the hot afternoon sun. Note the pass-through between the kitchen and family room. The rear terrace is stepped to accommodate the sunken living room.

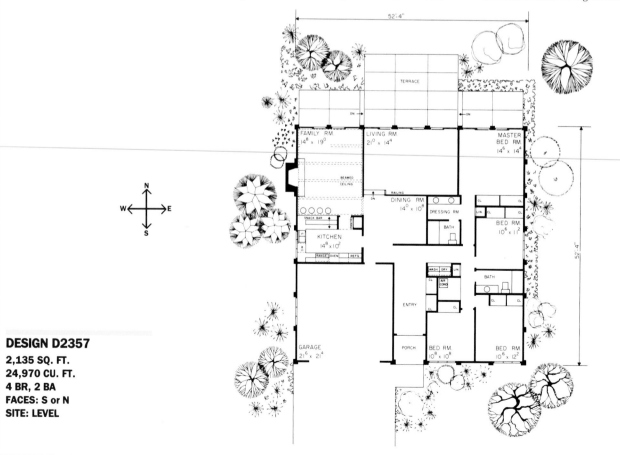

DESIGN D2357
2,135 SQ. FT.
24,970 CU. FT.
4 BR, 2 BA
FACES: S or N
SITE: LEVEL

This Spanish-style rambler is reminiscent of the Southwest but would work in any region of the country. In cool or moderate areas, the back should face south to admit direct sunlight into the master bedroom, living room, and dining room. The east and west sides have few windows for efficient cooling, and the north features a sheltered entryway. Note that the three bedrooms are clustered together and separated from the spacious living and dining area. The kitchen and nook have a view of the entry walkway. The kitchen has abundant storage space. In hot regions the front of the home should face south so the daytime living areas are sheltered from direct sunshine.

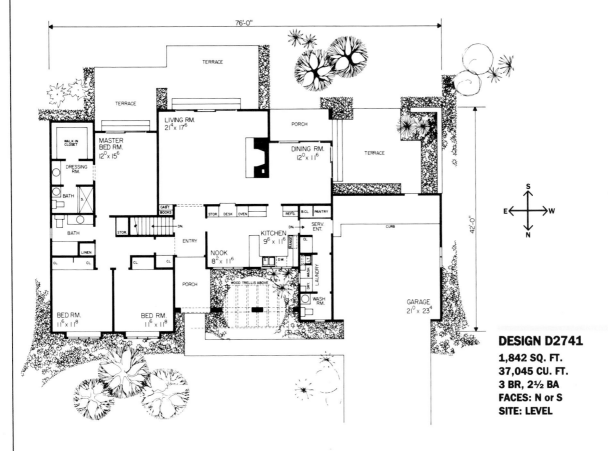

DESIGN D2741
1,842 SQ. FT.
37,045 CU. FT.
3 BR, 2½ BA
FACES: N or S
SITE: LEVEL

Skylights and Clerestories

Soaring gable windows on the west side, numerous skylights, and large glass areas on the south side ensure a bright and sunny interior for this delightful contemporary. The master bedroom, study, and family room receive direct winter sun. A screened porch on the south side, with skylights, offers outdoor living in any kind of weather. The garage protects it from direct west sun. There are few windows on the east side. This plan could work in reverse also, with the entrance facing east, to avoid late afternoon sunshine through the front windows. Note the private terrace and the pool off the master bedroom, and the skylights over the whirlpool tub in the master bath.

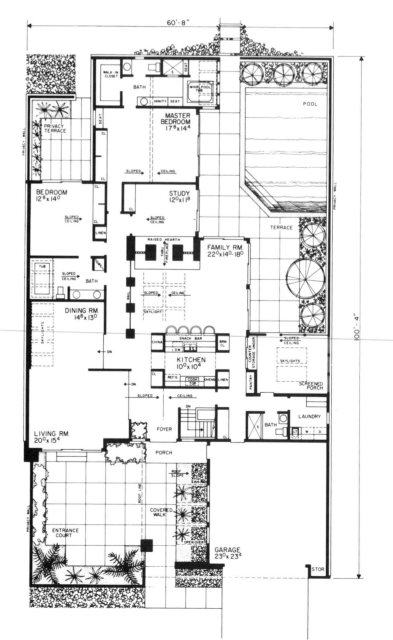

DESIGN D2882
2,832 SQ. FT.
59,635 CU. FT.
2 BR, 3 BA + STUDY
FACES: W
SITE: LEVEL

This split-level contemporary features two interior planters. One of them, just inside the front entry, is set off dramatically by soaring windows and a skylight. The study area of the master bedroom overlooks this space from above. Windows and glass doors on the south wall let winter sunlight into the breakfast and kitchen area, dining room, living room, and master bedroom — and also into the downstairs family room and bedroom, depending on how much the sun is blocked by decks. The kitchen and living room also receive morning sun. One downstairs bedroom and the study have windows facing west. Note the basement's flexible arrangement of space.

DESIGN D2679
3,183 SQ. FT.
43,733 CU. FT.
3 BR, 3 BA + STUDY
FACES: N
SITE: SLOPES SW

Two spacious family rooms downstairs and the upstairs master bedroom receive most of the winter sunshine in this contemporary plan, but a large ridge skylight over the main gathering room provides the most dramatic light. Because part of the skylight slopes to the south, it receives some direct sunlight in winter; in the summer, it should be shaded to prevent overheating. The gathering room also receives morning sunlight through an east window, and the activity room receives late afternoon sunlight through a west window. Note the convenient placement of the kitchen and eating nook, adjacent to the entry, and with a view into the central atrium.

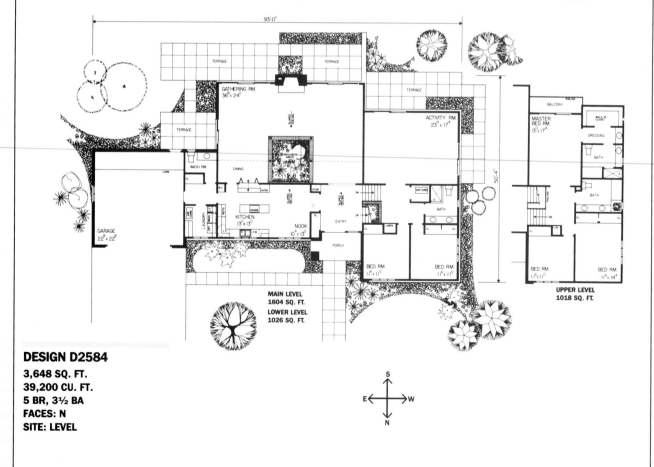

DESIGN D2584
3,648 SQ. FT.
39,200 CU. FT.
5 BR, 3½ BA
FACES: N
SITE: LEVEL

This spacious contemporary features a three-story open space topped by a bank of skylights. Surrounded by balconies on the main and upper levels, this dramatic feature ties all three floors of this home together. It is an efficient and effective solution to the problems posed by sites where direct sunlight to the south side of the home is limited by hills, trees, or other obstacles. There are enough windows to admit daylight into some rooms, particularly on the north side, but the soaring well in the center of the home fills it with light from above. Note the few windows on the east and west sides and the dramatic two-story planter well on the south side of the house.

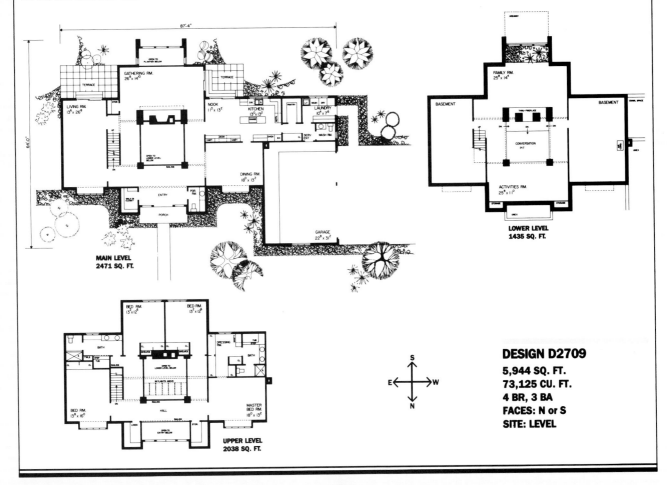

MAIN LEVEL
2471 SQ. FT.

LOWER LEVEL
1435 SQ. FT.

UPPER LEVEL
2038 SQ. FT.

DESIGN D2709
5,944 SQ. FT.
73,125 CU. FT.
4 BR, 3 BA
FACES: N or S
SITE: LEVEL

With three stories of windows in the back, this contemporary offers ideal solar exposure. Winter sunlight enters the main-level bedroom and activities room and the upper-level bedroom, and floods the gathering room through a two-story window wall. None of the rooms has windows that face east, but the dining room, sleeping loft, and gathering room have windows facing west. A reverse plan would solve the problem of hot afternoon sun and open these same spaces to the morning sun. Note how the decks shade several downstairs windows and how the clerestory windows bring northern light into the gathering room. Each bedroom has a bathroom of its own.

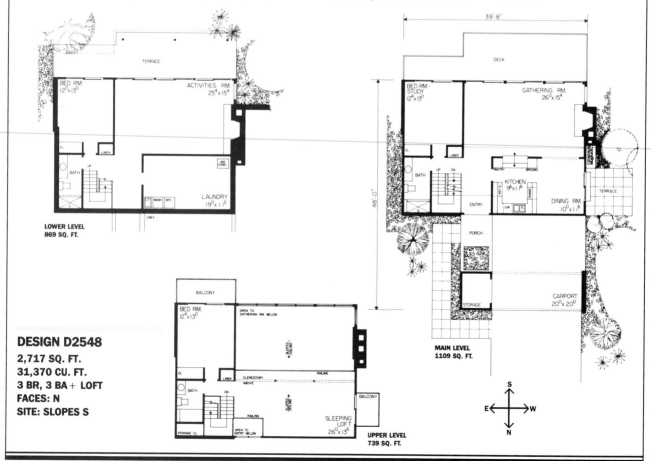

DESIGN D2548

2,717 SQ. FT.
31,370 CU. FT.
3 BR, 3 BA + LOFT
FACES: N
SITE: SLOPES S

LOWER LEVEL
869 SQ. FT.

UPPER LEVEL
739 SQ. FT.

MAIN LEVEL
1109 SQ. FT.

Three skylights brighten the foyer of this hillside contemporary. They slope toward the north, providing daylight without the direct sun that could cause overheating. The back of the home opens to the south for ideal solar exposure in the winter. The study, gathering room, dining room, breakfast area, and downstairs rooms all receive direct sun. The bathrooms, closets, laundry, and garage are on the north side of the home to buffer against winter storms. Note the wells alongside the stairway that let light from the skylights all the way into the basement.

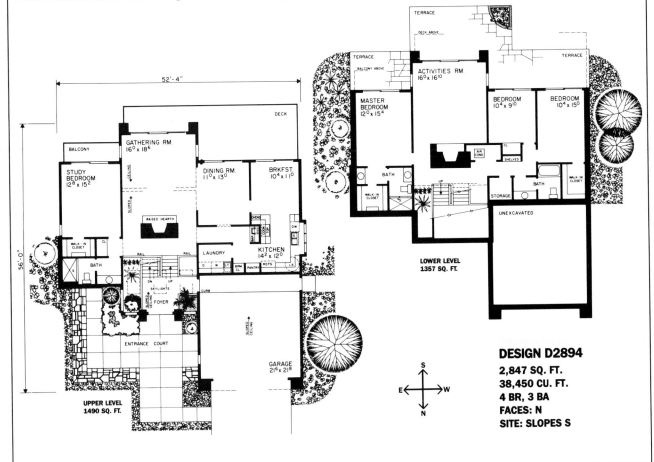

DESIGN D2894
2,847 SQ. FT.
38,450 CU. FT.
4 BR, 3 BA
FACES: N
SITE: SLOPES S

Skylights next to the chimney add dramatic appeal to the living and dining rooms of this split-level contemporary. Large windows on the east wall of the living room flood it with morning sunlight. The dining room, kitchen, breakfast room, family room, and master bedroom receive sun throughout winter days, and two bedrooms have west windows for the late afternoon sun. One bedroom over the garage has a north window, its own balcony, and easy access to the front door, making it ideal for a home office. Note the sunken living room and family room with sliding doors to the terrace. The covered porch outside the kitchen is perfect for summer meals.

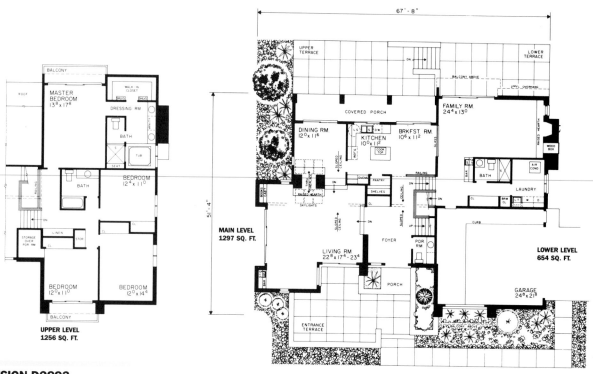

UPPER LEVEL
1256 SQ. FT.

MAIN LEVEL
1297 SQ. FT.

LOWER LEVEL
654 SQ. FT.

DESIGN D2893
3,207 SQ. FT.
49,198 CU. FT.
4 BR, 3½ BA
FACES: N
SITE: SLOPES W

The rooms along the back of this handsome contemporary— master bedroom, drawing room, gathering room, nook, and kitchen — all have a southern exposure for direct winter sunshine, but the most striking feature is a two-story light well in the center of the home. It has a skylight directly overhead, supplementing the sunshine that streams in through the south-facing windows and doors. The east and west sides have only one window, except for side windows on the gathering room, and the garage buffers the north-west corner of the home. The main living spaces all open to the back. Note how the garage shades the dining room from late afternoon sun in the peak of summer.

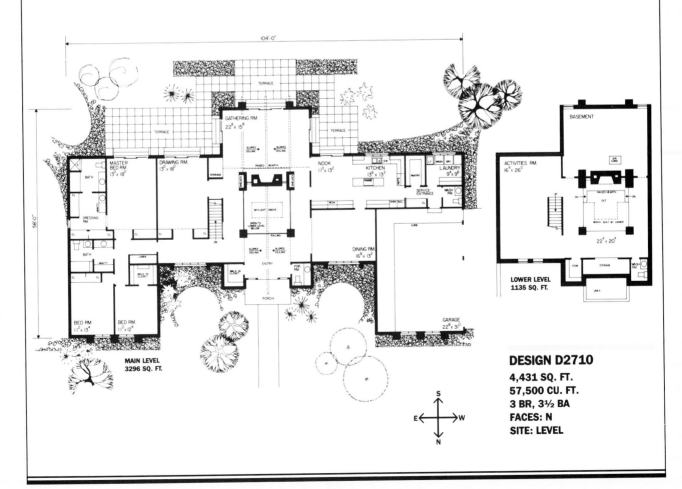

DESIGN D2710

4,431 SQ. FT.
57,500 CU. FT.
3 BR, 3½ BA
FACES: N
SITE: LEVEL

A central skylight brightens the foyer and living areas of this hillside contemporary. Large windows on the south side bring winter sunlight directly into the breakfast room, dining room, living room, family room, master bedroom, and downstairs rooms. Balconies and a stepped profile shade some of the windows during certain times of the day. The kitchen and breakfast room receive morning sunlight, and windows next to the whirlpool tub in the master bathroom face west for afternoon sun. Note the sloped ceilings in many of the rooms and the spacious entry foyer with a seating alcove beneath the skylight.

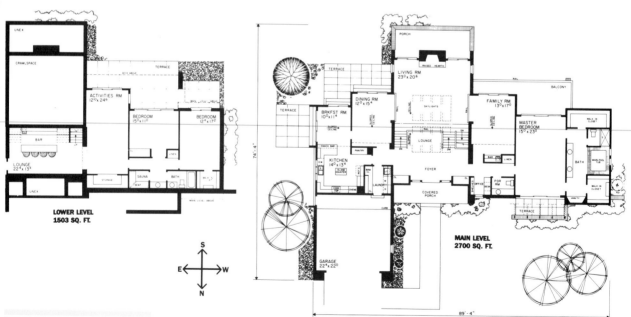

**LOWER LEVEL
1503 SQ. FT.**

**MAIN LEVEL
2700 SQ. FT.**

DESIGN D2895
4,203 SQ. FT.
54,645 CU. FT.
3 BR, 2½ BA
FACES: N
SITE: SLOPES SW

Designing with Solar Collectors

A sunspace across the entire back of this solar home creates an exotic grotto in the winter and produces heat for all the main living spaces. Solar collectors could easily be installed on the south-facing roof. The kitchen, tucked into the northwest corner, has a window facing west and is buffered on the north side by the garage. The lower level receives abundant sunlight from the solarium skylights. Note the raised bathtub in the master bathroom, and the upper-level balcony overlooking the solarium with its whirlpool spa.

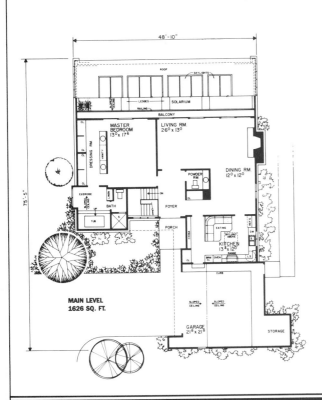

MAIN LEVEL
1626 SQ. FT.

LOWER LEVEL
2038 SQ. FT.

DESIGN D2835
3,664 SQ. FT.
50,926 CU. FT.
3 BR, 3½ BA
FACES: N
SITE: SLOPES S

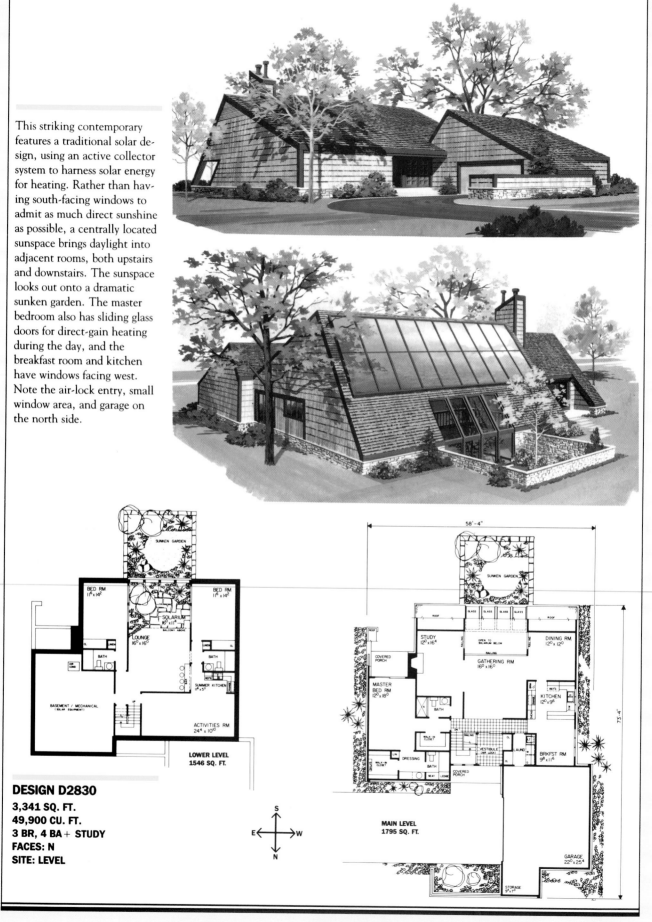

This striking contemporary features a traditional solar design, using an active collector system to harness solar energy for heating. Rather than having south-facing windows to admit as much direct sunshine as possible, a centrally located sunspace brings daylight into adjacent rooms, both upstairs and downstairs. The sunspace looks out onto a dramatic sunken garden. The master bedroom also has sliding glass doors for direct-gain heating during the day, and the breakfast room and kitchen have windows facing west. Note the air-lock entry, small window area, and garage on the north side.

DESIGN D2830
3,341 SQ. FT.
49,900 CU. FT.
3 BR, 4 BA + STUDY
FACES: N
SITE: LEVEL

LOWER LEVEL
1546 SQ. FT.

MAIN LEVEL
1795 SQ. FT.

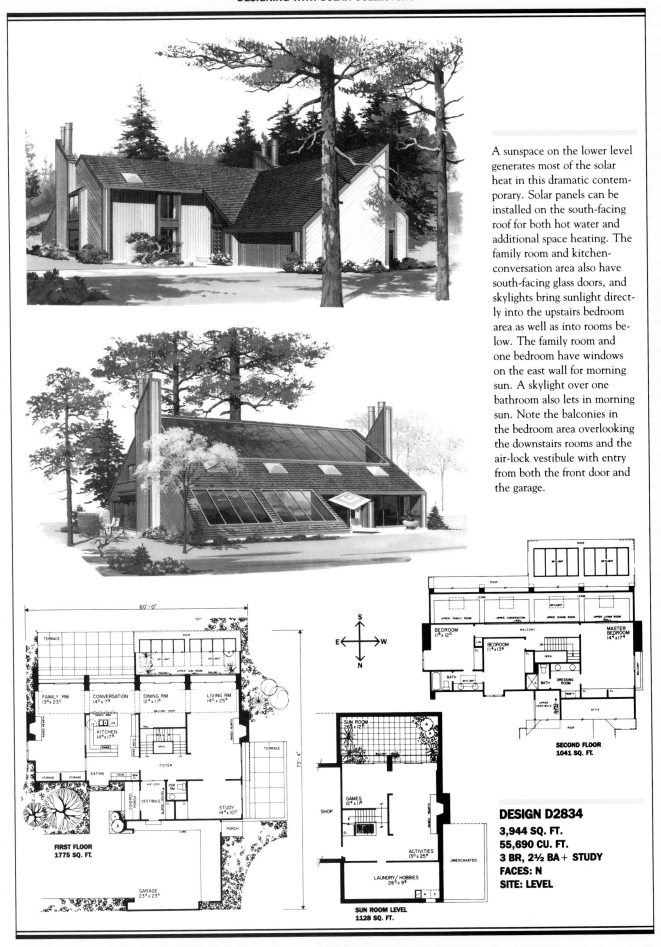

A sunspace on the lower level generates most of the solar heat in this dramatic contemporary. Solar panels can be installed on the south-facing roof for both hot water and additional space heating. The family room and kitchen-conversation area also have south-facing glass doors, and skylights bring sunlight directly into the upstairs bedroom area as well as into rooms below. The family room and one bedroom have windows on the east wall for morning sun. A skylight over one bathroom also lets in morning sun. Note the balconies in the bedroom area overlooking the downstairs rooms and the air-lock vestibule with entry from both the front door and the garage.

DESIGN D2834
3,944 SQ. FT.
55,690 CU. FT.
3 BR, 2½ BA + STUDY
FACES: N
SITE: LEVEL

The Design Category Series

(1)

210 ONE STORY HOMES OVER 2,000 SQUARE FEET Spacious homes for gracious living. Includes all popular styles — Spanish, Western, Tudor, French, Contemporary, and others. Amenity-filled plans feature master bedroom suites, atriums, courtyards, and pools. **192 pages. $4.95 ($5.95 Canada)**

(2)

315 ONE STORY HOMES UNDER 2,000 SQUARE FEET Economical homes in a variety of styles. Efficient floor plans contain plenty of attractive features — gathering rooms, formal and informal living and dining rooms, mudrooms, outdoor living spaces, and more. Many plans are expandable. **192 pages. $4.95 ($5.95 Canada)**

(3)

150 1½ STORY HOMES From starter homes to country estates. Includes classic story-and-a-half styles: Contemporary, Williamsburg, Georgian, Tudor, and Cape Cod. Outstanding outdoor livability. Many expandable plans. **128 pages. $3.95 ($4.95 Canada)**

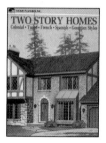

(4)

360 TWO STORY HOMES Plans for all budgets and all families, in a wide range of styles: Tudors, Saltboxes, Farmhouses, Southern Colonials, Georgians, Contemporaries, and more. Many plans have extra-large kitchens, extra bedrooms, and extra baths. **263 pages. $6.95 ($8.95 Canada)**

(5)

215 MULTI-LEVEL HOMES Distinctive styles for both flat and sloping sites. Tailor-made for great outdoor living. Features include exposed lower levels, upper-level lounges, balconies, decks, and terraces. Includes plans for all building budgets. **192 pages. $4.95 ($5.95 Canada)**

(6)

223 VACATION HOMES Full-color volume features A-frames, chalets, lodges, hexagons, cottages, and other attractive styles in one-story, two-story, and multi-level plans ranging from 480 to 3,238 square feet. Perfect for woodland, lakeside, or seashore. **176 pages. $4.95 ($5.95 Canada)**

Other Current Titles

(7)

TUDOR HOUSES Here is the stuff that dream houses are made of! A superb portfolio of 80 enchanting Tudor-style homes, from cozy Cotswold cottages to impressive Baronial manors. Includes a decorating section filled with colorful photographs and illustrations showing 24 different furniture arrangements. **208 pages. $10.95 paperback ($12.95 Canada)**

(8)

COUNTRY HOUSES Shows off 80 gorgeous country homes in three eye-catching styles: Cape Cods, Farmhouses, and Center-Hall Colonials. Each house features an architect's exterior rendering, artist's depiction of a furnished interior room, large floor plans, and adorable decorating schemes for nine different country-style rooms. **208 pages. $10.95 ($12.95 Canada)**

(9)

HOME PLANS FOR OUTDOOR LIVING This superbly produced book showcases more than 100 plans, each uniquely styled to bring the outdoors in. Features terraces, decks, porches, balconies, courtyards, atriums, and sunspaces. Includes brilliant full-color photography of homes actually built and down-to-earth planning pointers. **192 pages. $10.95 ($12.95 Canada)**

Please fill out the coupon below. We will process your order and ship it from our office within 48 hours. Send coupon and check for the total to: **HOME PLANNERS, INC.**, 23761 Research Drive, Department BK, Farmington Hills, MI 48024

THE DESIGN CATEGORY SERIES

1. _____ 210 One Story Homes over 2,000 Square Feet @ $4.95 ($5.95 Canada) $ _____

2. _____ 315 One Story Homes Under 2,000 Square Feet @ $4.95 ($5.95 Canada) $ _____

3. _____ 150 1½ Story Homes @ $3.95 ($4.95 Canada) $ _____

4. _____ 360 Two Story Homes @ $6.95 ($8.95 Canada) $ _____

5. _____ 215 Multi-Level Homes @ $4.95 ($5.95 Canada) $ _____

6. _____ 223 Vacation Homes @ $4.95 ($5.95 Canada) $ _____

OTHER CURRENT TITLES

7. _____ Tudor Houses @ $10.95 ($12.95 Canada) $ _____

8. _____ Country Houses @ $10.95 ($12.95 Canada) $ _____

9. _____ Home Plans for Outdoor Living @ $10.95 ($12.95 Canada) $ _____

Subtotal $ _____

Michigan residents: Add 4% sales tax $ _____

Add postage and handling $ 1.50

TOTAL (please enclose check) $ _____

Name (please print) _____

Address _____

City _____ State _____ Zip _____

CANADIAN CUSTOMERS: Please use Canadian prices noted. Remit in Canadian funds to: Home Planners, Inc., 20 Cedar St. North, Kitchener, Ontario N2H 2W8 Phone: (519) 743-4169

TB13BK

The Basic Blueprint Package

Building a home? Planning a home? The Basic Blueprint Package from Home Planners, Inc., contains nearly everything you need to get the job done right, whether you're working on your own or with help from an architect, designer, builder, or subcontractors. Each Basic Blueprint Package includes detailed architect's blueprints and a specification outline.

Each set of blueprints is an interrelated collection of plans, measurements, drawings, and diagrams showing precisely how your house comes together. Here's what it includes.

FRONTAL SHEET. An artist's landscaped sketch of the exterior, along with ink-line floor plans.

FOUNDATION PLAN. A complete basement and foundation plan in ¼-inch scale, plus a sample plot plan for locating your house on a building site.

DETAILED FLOOR PLANS. Drawn to ¼-inch scale, each floor plan includes cross-section detail keys and layouts of electrical outlets and switches.

HOUSE CROSS SECTIONS. Large-scale views show key sections of the foundation, interior and exterior walls, floors, and roof details.

INTERIOR ELEVATIONS. Large-scale interior details show the design of kitchen cabinets, bathrooms, laundry areas, fireplaces, and built-ins.

EXTERIOR ELEVATIONS. Drawings in ¼-inch scale show the front, rear, and sides of your house.

SPECIFICATION LIST. Every Basic Blueprint Package also includes a 16-page, fill-in-the-items specification list containing more than 150 stages crucial to building a house correctly, from excavating to painting. A handy guide and record, it allows you to pinpoint building materials, equipment, and methods of construction.

Important Extras

Home Planners, Inc., offers a variety of other products aimed at helping you plan, build, and design your new home. These include Materials List, Plumbing Details, Construction Details, Electrical Details, and the Plan-A-Home™ Package.

Materials List

If you choose, we can provide a materials take-off for your plan. An important part of the building package, this list outlines the quantity, type, and size of everything needed to build your house (with the exception of mechanical materials). Included are:

- masonry, veneer, and fireplace;
- framing lumber;
- roofing and sheet metal;
- windows and door frames;
- exterior trim;
- insulation;
- tile and flooring;
- interior trim;
- kitchen cabinets;
- rough and finish hardware.

The list, which you pay for only once no matter how many blueprints you order, is not only a directory of the products destined for your house, it's a useful tool as well. It can help you cost out materials and serve as a handy reference sheet when you're compiling bids. And it can help coordinate the substitution of building materials when you need to meet local codes, use available supplies, satisfy personal preferences, and the like.

(Because of differing codes and methods of installation, our lists don't include mechanical materials and specifications. To get the necessary take-offs, consult local heating, plumbing, and electrical contractors or a local lumberyard or building supply center. Materials lists are not sold separately from the Blueprint Package.)

Plumbing Details

The Basic Blueprint Package includes locations for all the plumbing fixtures in your house, including sinks, lavatories, tubs, showers, toilets, laundry trays, and water heaters. If you want to find out more about the intricacies of household plumbing, these 24 × 36-inch drawings — six individual, fact-packed sheets — will prove to be remarkably useful tools. Prepared to meet requirements of the National Plumbing Code, these valuable Plumbing Details show pipe schedules, fittings, sump-pump details, water-softener hookups, septic system details, and much more. Sheets are bound together and color coded for easy reference. A glossary of terms is included.

Construction Details

The Basic Blueprint Package contains everything an experienced builder needs to construct a particular plan. However, it doesn't show all the different ways building materials come together to form a house, or all construction techniques used by skilled artisans. To show you a variety of additional techniques and materials, we also offer a complete set of detail drawings that depict — in an exquisitely precise way — the materials and methods used to build foundations, fireplaces, walls, floors, and roofs.

What's more, where appropriate, the drawings depict acceptable alternatives. For the advanced do-it-yourselfer, owner-builder-to-be, or inquisitive home planner, these construction details are the perfect complement to the basic package.

Electrical Details

The Basic Blueprint Package shows positions for every electrical switch, plug, and outlet. However, our Electrical Details go further to take the mystery out of household electrical systems. These comprehensive 24 × 36-inch drawings come packed with helpful details. Prepared to meet requirements of the National Electrical Code, the six fact-filled sheets cover a variety of topics including appliance wattage, wire sizing, switch-installation schematics, cable-routing details, doorbell hookups, and much more. Sheets are bound together and color coded for easy reference. A glossary of terms is also included.

Our plumbing, electrical, and construction details can be remarkably useful tools. Although we don't recommend that you attempt intricate plumbing or electrical installations, or complicated building projects, these drawings will help you accomplish certain tasks and will give you and your family a thorough working knowledge with which to deal confidently with subcontractors.

Plan-A-Home™

Plan-A-Home™ is a very useful tool. It's an easy-to-use product that will help you design a new home, arrange furniture in a new or existing home, or plan a remodeling project. Each package contains:

- more than 700 accurate planning symbols on a vinyl sheet, including walls, windows, doors, furniture, kitchen components, bath fixtures, and much more. All are made of a durable, peel-and-stick vinyl you can use over and over;
- a reusable, transparent, ¼-inch-scale planning grid that can help you create house layouts up to 140 × 92 feet;
- tracing paper and a protective separating sheet;
- a flexible planning ruler;
- a felt-tip pen, with water-soluble ink that wipes away quickly.

The transparent planning grid matches the scale of actual working blueprints (¼ inch equals 1 foot). You can lay it over existing drawings and modify them as necessary, or plan furniture arrangements before you build. Every Plan-A-Home™ package lets you lay out areas as large as a 7,500-square-foot, six-bedroom, seven-bath home. Note, however, that Plan-A-Home™ isn't meant to replace construction drawings. When you've planned a building project, consult an architect, designer, or contractor for help.

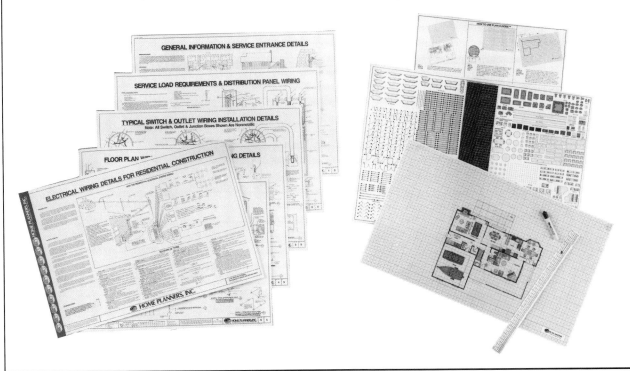

Price Schedule

THE BASIC BLUEPRINT PACKAGE

The blueprints you order are a master plan for building your new home as well as an education in building techniques. Even the smallest house in the Home Planners portfolio is a complicated combination of construction data and architectural detailing. Bigger houses, irregularly shaped houses, and houses with an abundance of design features are even more complex and require proportionately greater resources to plan and develop. The schedule below takes these factors into account when pricing each of the plans. To fill out an order, note the index letter (A, B, C, or D) next to the plan number in the index below, and refer to the appropriate prices in the following schedule.

	Single Set	Four-Set Package	Eight-Set Package	Sepias
Schedule A	$125.00	$175.00	$225.00	$250.00
Schedule B	$150.00	$200.00	$250.00	$300.00
Schedule C	$175.00	$225.00	$275.00	$350.00
Schedule D	$200.00	$250.00	$300.00	$400.00

Additional Identical Blueprints in Same Order: $30.00 per set.
Reverse Blueprints: $30.00 per order.
Additional Specification Outlines: $5.00 per outline.

IMPORTANT EXTRAS

Materials List ....$25.00 (for any size order)

Construction
Details $14.95

Plumbing Details $14.95

Electrical Details $14.95

Two-Set Package:
Any Two of Construction,
Plumbing, and Electrical Details ....$22.95 (save $6.95)

Three-Set Package:
Construction, Plumbing,
and Electrical Details ....$29.95 (save $14.90)

Plan-A-Home™ $24.95

Plans and Price Index

KEY: **D1220** is the plan number. **137** is the page on which the plan appears. **(B)** is the price index letter.

D1220, 137 (B)	D2392, 149 (D)	D2664, 156 (B)	D2741, 169 (B)	D2832, 112 (C)	D2873, 124 (C)	D2906, 83 (C)
D1223, 92 (C)	D2431, 114 (A)	D2668, 113 (B)	D2760, 150 (C)	D2834, 181 (D)	D2880, 128 (C)	D2909, 107 (B)
D1264, 139 (D)	D2472, 105 (A)	D2669, 144 (B)	D2763, 80 (C)	D2835, 179 (C)	D2881, 142 (C)	D2915, 134 (C)
D1443, 95 (C)	D2485, 147 (B)	D2670, 165 (D)	D2767, 94 (D)	D2839, 129 (C)	D2882, 170 (C)	D2917, 167 (B)
D2135, 104 (C)	D2509, 140 (C)	D2679, 171 (C)	D2769, 86 (C)	D2841, 82 (B)	D2883, 132 (C)	D2921, 127 (D)
D2251, 91 (A)	D2534, 93 (D)	D2680, 153 (C)	D2774, 154 (B)	D2843, 135 (C)	D2884, 131 (B)	D2926, 106 (D)
D2254, 122 (C)	D2548, 174 (C)	D2686, 155 (C)	D2781, 136 (C)	D2844, 148 (C)	D2886, 125 (B)	D2933, 101 (D)
D2256, 81 (C)	D2549, 88 (C)	D2687, 130 (C)	D2795, 166 (B)	D2846, 162 (C)	D2893, 176 (C)	D2934, 89 (D)
D2266, 99 (C)	D2558, 111 (A)	D2692, 133 (C)	D2804, 164 (B)	D2850, 143 (C)	D2894, 175 (C)	D2937, 79 (C)
D2315, 145 (B)	D2580, 146 (C)	D2694, 152 (C)	D2823, 116 (B)	D2856, 87 (C)	D2895, 178 (D)	D2946, 138 (C)
D2327, 98 (B)	D2583, 141 (C)	D2695, 102 (C)	D2825, 100 (B)	D2857, 90 (D)	D2900, 119 (C)	
D2330, 163 (B)	D2584, 172 (C)	D2696, 161 (D)	D2826, 85 (B)	D2858, 108 (C)	D2901, 123 (C)	
D2343, 96 (B)	D2615, 117 (D)	D2699, 103 (D)	D2827, 120 (C)	D2863, 110 (C)	D2902, 126 (B)	
D2357, 168 (B)	D2650, 160 (B)	D2709, 173 (D)	D2830, 180 (C)	D2865, 157 (C)	D2904, 121 (C)	
D2386, 97 (B)	D2660, 158 (D)	D2710, 177 (D)	D2831, 109 (C)	D2871, 118 (B)	D2905, 84 (B)	

Before You Order

Just clip the accompanying order blank and mail with your remittance. If you prefer, you can also use a credit card or order C.O.D. (Sorry, we aren't allowed to make C.O.D. shipments to foreign countries, including Canada.) If time is of the essence, call us. We'll ship orders received before 3 p.m. Eastern time the following day. Use this toll-free number: 1-800-521-6797. (Michigan residents call collect: 0-313-477-1850.) If you use the coupon, please note applicable postage and handling charges.

OUR SERVICE POLICY We try to process and ship every order from our office within 48 hours. For this reason, we won't send a formal notice acknowledging receipt of your order.

OUR EXCHANGE POLICY Since blueprints are printed in response to your order, we cannot honor requests for refunds. However, we will exchange your entire first order for an equal number of blueprints at a price of $20.00 for the first set and $10.00 for each additional set. All sets from the previous order must be returned before the exchange can take place. Please add $3.00 for postage and handling via surface mail; $4.00 via air mail.

ABOUT REVERSE BLUEPRINTS If you want to build in reverse of the plan as shown, we will upon request include an extra set of reversed blueprints for an additional fee of $30.00. Although letters and dimensions appear backward, reverses will prove to be a useful visual aid if you decide to flop the plan.

MODIFYING OUR PLANS Slight revisions are easy to do before you start building. (We don't alter plans, by the way.) If you're thinking about major changes, consider ordering a set of sepias. After changes have been made on the sepia, additional sets of plans may be reproduced from the sepia master. Should you decide to revise the plan significantly, we strongly suggest that you consult an experienced architect or designer.

HOW MANY BLUEPRINTS DO YOU NEED? From one to eight sets—sometimes more. To study your favorite house (or houses) in greater detail, one set is sufficient. On the other hand, if you plan to build, you need more. Because the first set of blueprints in each order is the scheduled price and because extra sets of the same design are only $30.00 each, you save a lot of money by ordering all the required sets at one time. Use the following checklist to estimate the total.

_____ **Owner**
_____ **Builder** (generally requires a minimum of three sets: one to use as a legal document, one to use during inspections, and at least one to give to tradespeople)
_____ **Community Building Department** (often requires two sets)
_____ **Mortgage Lender** (to make a conventional loan, usually one set; to process government-insured or approved loans, three sets)
_____ **Subdivision Committee**
_____ **Planning Commission**
_____ **TOTAL NUMBER OF SETS**

TO ORDER BLUEPRINTS BY PHONE Call toll free: 1-800-521-6797. Michigan residents call collect: 0-313-477-1850. If we get your order by 3 p.m. Eastern time, we'll process it the same day and ship it to you from our office the following day. Call to order blueprints or books only. **PLEASE NOTE:** When you order by phone, we'll ask for the Order Form Key. It's located in the lower left-hand corner of the order form on this page.

CANADIAN CUSTOMERS Please add 20% to all prices, and mail in Canadian funds to: HOME PLANNERS, INC.; 20 Cedar St. North; Kitchener, Ontario N2H 2W8. Phone: (519) 743-4169.

Order Form

SEND TO:

 HOME PLANNERS, INC.
23761 RESEARCH DRIVE
FARMINGTON HILLS, MICHIGAN 48024

THE BASIC BLUEPRINT PACKAGE Rush me the following (please refer to the Plans Index and Schedule Price opposite):

_____ Set(s) of blueprints for plan number(s)
_____ $ _____
_____ Set(s) of sepias for plan number(s)
_____ $ _____
_____ Additional identical blueprints in same order
@ $30.00 per set $ _____
_____ Reverse blueprints @ $30.00 per order $ _____
_____ Additional Specification Outlines @ $5.00 each $ _____

IMPORTANT EXTRAS Rush me the following

_____ **Materials List** @ $25.00 (any size order) $ _____
_____ **Construction Details** @ $14.95 each $ _____
_____ **Plumbing Details** @ $14.95 each $ _____
_____ **Electrical Details** @ $14.95 each $ _____
_____ **Two-Set Package** @ $22.95 (save $6.95).
Please indicate any two of Construction, Plumbing, and Electrical Details. $ _____
_____ **Three-Set Package** @ $29.95 (save $14.90).
Includes Construction, Plumbing, and Electrical Details. $ _____
_____ **Plan-A-Home™** @ $24.95 each $ _____

FOR POSTAGE AND HANDLING

_____ $3.00 added to order for surface mail (UPS; any merchandise) $ _____
_____ $5.00 added for priority mail of 1 to 4 sets of blueprints $ _____
_____ $8.00 added for priority mail of 5 or more sets of blueprints $ _____
_____ For Canadian orders, add $2.00 to applicable rates above $ _____
_____ C.O.D. (Pay mail carrier; U.S. only)

TOTAL in U.S. funds (Michigan residents add 4% sales tax) $ _____

YOUR ADDRESS (please print)

Name _____

Street _____

City _____ State _____ ZIP _____

Daytime telephone number (_____) _____

FOR CREDIT CARD ORDERS ONLY Please fill in the boxes below:

Credit card number   Exp. Date: Month/Year

Check one   ☐ MasterCard   ☐ VISA

Signature _____

TB13BP

Glossary

ACTIVE SOLAR   Heating and cooling strategies that rely on the collection, storage, and distribution of solar energy in the form of heat by active components such as pumps, ducts, collectors, and heat exchangers.

AIR EXCHANGE   The complete replacement of interior air with fresh outdoor air, specified at a rate of so many exchanges per hour.

AIR-LOCK ENTRY (WEATHERLOCK ENTRY)   A small entry room shut off from the rest of the house by an interior door that can remain shut while the door to the outside is open.

ATRIUM   A garden area surrounded by living areas of the home. It can be either open to the sky or covered by a skylight.

BERM HOME   A home with earth piled against some exterior walls for increased insulation.

BTU   British thermal unit. The amount of heat required to raise the temperature of one pound of water by one degree Fahrenheit.

BUFFER   An auxiliary space, such as a garage, closet, or laundry room, that separates the main living areas from extreme climatic conditions.

CAULKING   Material used for sealing exterior cracks and seams to prevent air and moisture leaks.

CLERESTORY WINDOW   A vertical window placed between two sloping roof sections of different heights, which brings daylight into the upper portions of interior rooms.

CONDUCTION   The transfer of heat through a solid material.

CONVECTION   The transfer of heat by moving air.

CONVECTIVE LOOP (CONVECTOR LOOP)   A circular path of moving air created by the upward movement of air as it is heated and the downward movement of the air as it cools.

DIRECT SOLAR GAIN   The heating of a space by sun shining directly into the space through windows or skylights.

DOUBLE-GLAZED WINDOWS   Windows that have two layers of glass separated by an air space and sealed around the edges.

EARTH-SHELTERED HOME   A home with earth placed against the walls and over the roof to increase insulation.

ENERGY-EFFICIENT DESIGN   Design features that use energy for heating, lighting, and other functions with a minimum of waste.

HEAT EXCHANGER (AIR-TO-AIR HEAT EXCHANGER)   A device that uses the heat from indoor air that is being exhausted to warm the incoming outdoor air that replaces it, without direct contact between the two air streams.

HOUSE WRAP   A special membrane used to wrap the outside of a home before the siding is installed. It seals against air leaks, drafts, and dust, but allows unwanted moisture to escape from wall cavities.

INDIRECT SOLAR GAIN   The warming of a space with solar heat captured in some other medium, such as air or fluid circulated in a collector, or a concrete wall.

INSULATION   Lightweight material placed inside the walls, floor, and ceiling of a building to resist the transfer of heat. Insulation is used to keep the inside of a building warmer or cooler than the outside, depending on the season.

LOW-E GLASS   Glass with a special coating that allows the transmission of solar heat into the living space but resists the loss of heat back out through the window.

MEAN RADIANT TEMPERATURE   The mean, or average, temperature of all the surfaces and objects in a space. Our bodies perceive this temperature, as well as that of the air, to form an overall comfort sensation.

MICROCLIMATE   The specific temperatures, breezes, shade patterns, and sunfall that occur in a particular neighborhood or building site.

MOVABLE INSULATION   Foam shutters, quilted shades, and similar devices that are placed over a window at night and on cold days to reduce heat loss.

ORIENTATION   The position of a home on its building site. This usually refers to the direction the front of the house or front door faces.

PASSIVE SOLAR   Heating and cooling strategies that rely on elements incorporated into the structure of the home, such as orientation, room layout, placement of windows, use of shading devices, and use of thermal mass materials, rather than on conventional heating and cooling systems that use electricity or fossil fuels.

PHASE-CHANGE MATERIALS   A chemical substance that stores heat more effectively than common building materials.

RADIANT HEAT   Heat transferred directly from a warmer to a cooler body without the intermediate air being warmed.

R-VALUE   A numerical measurement of insulation capability, referring to the ability of a material to resist heat transfer. The higher the R-value, the greater the resistance.

SOLAR ACCESS (SUN EXPOSURE POTENTIAL RATING)   The extent to which a site receives sunshine during various times of the year.

SOLAR CHIMNEY   An enclosed space with south-facing windows that collects large amounts of solar heat, which then causes currents of air to rise quickly.

SOLAR COLLECTOR   A device in which circulating air, water, or other fluid is heated by the sun; usually a flat panel mounted on the roof or other sunny location.

SOLAR GAIN   The amount of heat from the sun that is received in a passive solar home before heat loss is taken into account.

STRATIFICATION   The tendency of air to form layers based on temperature differences, with the warmest layer at the ceiling and the coolest at the floor.

SUN ANGLE   The angle of the sun's position in relation to the horizon; also called altitude.

SUNSPACE (ATTACHED GREENHOUSE; SOLARIUM; SUNROOM)   A room with south-facing windows and, sometimes, skylights for concentrating solar heat gain in one area: used as an indoor-outdoor living space and usually isolated from the rest of the house by doors.

SUPER INSULATION   A technique of constructing homes with extra-thick walls, ceilings, and floors to accommodate insulation of R-60 or more for ceilings and R-40 or more for walls.

THERMAL MASS   Dense building materials, such as tile, concrete, brick, stone, or water-filled containers used to absorb and store heat.

VAPOR BARRIER   A membrane of plastic or a similarly impermeable material that prevents moisture vapor inside the living space from migrating through the interior wall and ceiling surfaces and condensing on structural members inside the attic or wall.

VENTILATION   The replacement of interior air with fresh exterior air. Also, air movement inside crawl spaces and attics that impedes the growth of rot-causing fungus.

WEATHERSTRIPPING   Felt, foam, metal, or vinyl strips used to seal cracks around windows and doors that open to the outside.

WHOLE-HOUSE FAN   A large fan located in the ceiling of a central hallway that exhausts air from the home into the attic, helping to cool the interior and reduce the need for air conditioning.

WINDOW AREA   The total area of the glass panes in a house; does not include the wood or metal sash.

Bibliography

This bibliography lists a few of the many publications that will give you more ideas for living with the sun. In addition to the sources listed here, many local and government agencies can supply information about building houses with effective solar strategies. Try a local building department, energy commission, or utility company. University extensions and community colleges often offer courses in solar home building. In addition, the U.S. Government Printing Office and the National Association of Home Builders can supply you with a list of helpful publications.

Abrams, D.W., P.E. *Low-Energy Cooling: A Guide to the Practical Application of Passive Cooling on Cooling Energy Conservation Measures*. New York: Van Nostrand Reinhold Co., 1986.

Anderson, Bruce. *The New Solar Home Book*. Andover, MA: Brick House Publishers, 1987.

Anderson, Bruce, and Malcolm Wells. *Passive Solar Energy*. Andover, MA: Brick House Publishers, 1981.

Brown, G. Z. *Sun, Wind, and Light: Architectural Design Strategies*. New York: John Wiley & Sons, Inc., 1985.

California Energy Commission. *Energy Conservation Manual for New Residential Buildings*. Sacramento, CA: 1988.

Conklin, Groff, and S. Blackwell Duncan. *The Weather-Conditioned House*. New York: Van Nostrand Reinhold Co., rev. 1982.

Creech, Dennis B., and Jeffrey S. Tiller. *Building Guide for Energy-Smart Homes in Alabama*. Montgomery: Alabama Department of Economic and Community Affairs; Science, Technology, and Energy Division, 1988.

Crowley, John S., L. Zaurie Zimmerman, and Ralph J. Johnson. *Builder's Guide to Passive Solar Home Design and Land Development*. Topeka, KS: National Fenestration Council, 1983.

Franklin Research Center. *First Passive Solar Home Awards*. Philadelphia, PA, 1979.

Jones, R.W., and R.D. McFarland. *The Sun-Space Primer*. New York: Van Nostrand Reinhold, Co., 1984.

Mazria, Edward. *The Passive Solar Energy Book: A Complete Guide to Passive Solar Home, Greenhouse, and Building Design*. Emmaus, PA: Rodale Press, 1979.

Meltzer, M. *Passive and Active Solar Heating Technology*. Englewood Cliffs, NJ: Prentice-Hall, Inc.,1985.

Olgyay, Victor. *Design with Climate*. Princeton, NJ: Princeton University Press, 1963.

Robinette, G.O., and C. McClennon, eds. *Landscape Planning for Energy Conservation*. New York: Van Nostrand, Reinhold Co., 1983.

Schwolsky, Rick, and James I. Williams. *The Builder's Guide to Solar Construction*. New York: McGraw-Hill, 1982.

Smith, Ralph Lee. *Smart House: The Coming Revolution in Housing*. Columbia, MD: GP Publishing, 1988.

Watson, Donald. *Designing and Building a Solar House*. Rev. ed. Charlotte, VT: Garden Way Publications, 1985.

Index